G8

D0504306

An Axe, A Spade and Ten Acres

An Axe, A Spade and Ten Acres

 The story of a garden
and nature reserve

GEORGE COURTAULD

Illustrations and Maps by David Heal

Secker & Warburg

London

ESSEX LIBRARIES
LOCAL STUDIES DEPT.
COLCHESTER

DG 32757
E COL 4712.6

First published in England 1983 by
Martin Secker & Warburg Limited
54 Poland Street, London W1V 3DF

Copyright © 1983 by George Courtauld

British Library Cataloguing in Publication Data
Courtauld, George
 An axe, a spade and ten acres : the story of a
 garden and nature reserve.
 1. Gardens – Design   2. Gardening
 I. Title
 SB473·   712'.6

ISBN 0-436-10888-7

Photoset in Great Britain by
Rowland Phototypesetting Limited, Bury St. Edmunds, Suffolk
Printed by St Edmundsbury Press
Bury St Edmunds, Suffolk

List of Contents

MAPS

APPENDIXES

Contents

BARN

HOUSE

MEADOW
GARDEN

BACK LAWN

SILVER GARDEN

NUT GRO

ROSE
GARDEN

NEAR
POND

BLACK
POND

HERBACEOUS
BORDERS

THE RIDE

PINETUM

MANGROVE S

FIELD

PASTURE

FIELD

THE
BEAK

SMALL SCALE PLAN OF SITE

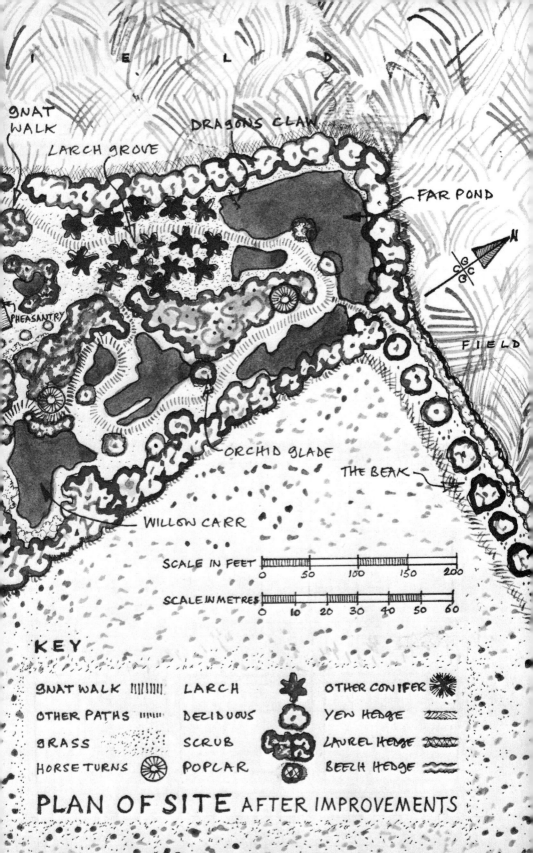

F I E L D

GNAT WALK

LARCH GROVE

DRAGONS CLAW

FAR POND

N

PHEASANTRY

FIELD

ORCHID GLADE

THE BEAK

WILLOW CARR

SCALE IN FEET

0   50   100   150   200

SCALE IN METRES

0   10   20   30   40   50   60

KEY

GNAT WALK	‖‖‖‖‖	LARCH		OTHER CONIFER	
OTHER PATHS	‖‖‖‖	DECIDUOUS		YEW HEDGE	
GRASS		SCRUB		LAUREL HEDGE	
HORSE TURNS		POPLAR		BEECH HEDGE	

PLAN OF SITE AFTER IMPROVEMENTS

View from North East of the whole site

CHAPTER 1

The Situation

Wastewood,
Nr Colchester,
Essex.
22nd May, 1982

To: The Editor of *The Morning Post*.

Dear Sir,

In view of the recent gloom about the falling standards of living, I suggest that there are only three necessities and three luxuries which are needed in life: the former being a spade, an axe and ten acres; the latter being an adequate supply of hot water, books and lavatory paper.

I am,

Yours sincerely,

George Courtauld

This book is the story of what I did with those three necessities, not, however, as a means of survival, but as an attempt to transform a hodge-podge of lawns and flower-beds, thickets and spinneys, swamps and ponds, pasture and woodland into a united garden and nature reserve. It is therefore not only the story of what was developed, cleared or planted, but also the story of what was left alone: the wild orchids, the kingfishers' nests, and the sheets of primroses by the rabbit warren. Like the garden, the book will ramble, it will wander off along diversionary paths, there may even be the occasional wet patch: it is very difficult to write about flowers without being winsome.

We live on the Essex-Suffolk border, an area of undulating agricultural land sandwiched between the Rivers Colne to the south and Stour to the north. Constable, a local man, painted the landscape two hundred years ago; nowadays there are fewer hedges and shaggy pastures, the water-mills are either forlorn or are inhabited by London commuters and the elms stand stag-headed or dead with Dutch disease; but still there exists the old painter's atmosphere of wide horizons and lush greenery. Two highly contrasting towns mark the extreme boundaries of east and west. The town on the east is Colchester, the oldest continuous garrison in the world: it was a fortress before the Romans arrived and soldiers still tramp the streets, now exchanging askance eyes with students from Essex University who lack-lustrely drift into town from their embattled concrete towers. Old King Coel was king of Colchester, then he was known as Cunobelin, changed by Shakespeare to Cymbeline; Boudicea, Queen of the neighbouring Icene, once hurtled through the garrison, burning the buildings and the Romans in them to crisps as she passed. The town to the west is Haverhill, formerly a pleasant market, but now much of it an aggressive clutter of mass-produced housing.

Around the two rivers and the two towns are sprinkled a collection of smaller villages and hamlets, some of whose names charm, like Finchingfield, Mount Bures, Steeple Bumpstead, White Ash Green and Countess Cross, and some whose names have a more homespun candour such as Rotten End, Foulslough, Slut's Green, Sewer's End and Dolt's.

After the decline of the medieval wool trade these cliquish villages slumbered quietly, unvisited by Londoners who had no wish to travel here on the appalling roads from the City: narrow, winding and dirty; crossing rivers with difficulty at Stamford, Ilford, Romford and Chelmsford. The train service which doddered out of Liverpool Street made little improvement, and so we never became fashionable and "civilised" like the other home counties. Now this has changed and the village populations are declining as the cottages, once crowded with families, are inhabited instead by weekenders, spruce from the London streets. However, part of the native population has remained static, based on agriculture and small local industries; our woodman, Bell, had only been to London once in seventy years:

"I went to Liverpool Street when I was a-courting, I couldn't abide the sight of it and took the next train home. Canon Holt asked me last year if I'd like a lift in his old car to see the sights of London and I said, 'Thank-ee Reverend, but I'd sooner ride a hedgehog to hell.'"

I have mentioned one local artist; Gainsborough was another. His wide-hipped, willowy and vacantly-gazing portraits resemble Midlanders rather than East Anglians: most of our natives are stocky, square-faced people, more like Yorkshiremen than any other of the English according to one survey of Britain; even their characters are similar and include such obscure twinning as a partiality for pork sausages and a high incidence of reckless driving.

Our house and garden stand on the edge of a plateau above the valley of one of the two rivers. Fields surround us but we can just see, on another plateau to the west, the encroaching walls of the small neighbouring town. Our village is out of sight in a hollow to the east and when looking towards the sunrise there is nothing higher than us, they say, than the spire of Warsaw Cathedral until one arrives at the Ural Mountains in Russia. In front of the house, to the south, the valley slopes the distance of three fields until it reaches the river. Northwards, the plateau extends to a wood mentioned in the Domesday Book and owned by a neighbour whose gamekeeper wages an undeclared war against Monk, my father's keeper. My parents live in the middle of our estate, Sam, my younger brother, lives over the river on its southernmost extremity and I live on the western boundary and am thus adjacent to the neighbour's fields.

The soil is immensely heavy yellow clay which lies as a mantle, from two to six feet deep, over several hundred feet of chalk. It is the sort of soil which can be cut into great solid blocks like squares of cheese, but which seems to weigh a ton when on the end of a spade: sometimes, when I try to toss it off the blade, it hangs sullenly on and nearly dislocates my arms. For about thirty years the site was used as a source for brick making and although the workings stopped in 1920 the clay diggings were still glaringly visible when we moved into the house in 1965: several of the ponds were straight-sided, showing that they were man-made rather than natural; there was a collection of large rectangular beds where the slurry of clay, chalk and grit was run to settle (having settled, the topmost layer of pure clay was moulded into bricks and baked for three weeks in slow-burning kilns); the remains of pug-mills and kilns still loom as earthern mounds twelve to fourteen feet above the surface of the garden.

Because of the chalk in the soil there is little chance of successfully growing acid-loving plants such as rhododendrons and heathers, but the massive size of the briars and old man's beard in the woodland is matched by their successful domestic counterparts, roses and clematis, in the formal parts of the garden.

When we moved in, we found that most of the area had not been touched for fifty years and so it had reverted to the original forest of old Essex; enough time had passed for oaks, elms and ashes to over-top a scratching tangle of thorn; clumps of hazel and the occasional silver birch lived in the lighter glades and, wherever there was a swamp or pond, a muddle of aspen and willows formed into what is known locally as a "carr"; many wild flowers, some now rare in the district, still grew in isolated pockets, and throughout the wood was my special heirloom, a mass of primroses such as I have never seen elsewhere. In the dark, overgrown thickets they lived sparsely and grew long-stemmed leaves and flowers which reached for the light, but once I had cleared glades they seeded and now blossom in closely packed yellow drifts.

Certain flowers sometimes take over an area and make it into their exclusive domain. Two miles away my father has a bluebell wood, in spring it is a shimmering haze of colour as if the trees were growing out of great patches of fallen sky; Dominie and I lived for three years by a wood in Yorkshire, and although it was famous for the ladies' slipper orchid I remember it most for its scented and snowy drifts of lily-of-the-valley.

As you can see on the map, the present shape of the garden is rather like the top half of a woodcock, with a long beak, a large eye, and a small head sloping to large shoulders. It extends for about 270 yards from north to south and averages 170 yards in width, excluding the Beak which is an extra 180 yards long. The total area is slightly over ten acres, of which nearly one-fifth is pond or swamp. It is bounded by fields except to the south where there is a small lane which meanders from the village to the town. The garden was originally smaller, the Pasture, the Beak and the Kitchen Garden being added to it since we moved in. There are fifteen distinct areas, namely:

1 *The Formal Garden* (0.8 acre)

This is the long and relatively narrow enclosure of approximately one hundred by forty yards which had been "gardened" around the house before we moved in. The inverted commas are used because it had not been touched for three years, except for the rose beds, and some parts had been unattended for even longer. From west to east it basically consists of the Kitchen Garden (some vegetable beds tucked beside the cart-lodge and stables), the entrance yard and house frontage with their assortment of flower borders, the Rose Garden enclosed by hedges of clipped yew, a crescent-shaped yew hedge with its fronting of flowers and gravel, two herbaceous borders running from the Rose Garden to the Pinetum, a shrubbery running parallel to their south and some fruit trees to the north.

2 *The Back Lawn* (0.5 acre)

Originally an area at the back of the house which was divided up by a muddle of rusted fencing, overgrown privet hedging and lines of cankered fruit trees; it included the remains of a kitchen garden, a chicken run and the grave-like mounds of abandoned flower-beds and compost heaps. It is now a wide expanse of lawn with an uncut area, the Meadow Garden, and a small copse of evergreens.

3 *The Near Pond* (0.14 acre)

The part of the garden I like best: I look at its heron-visited banks from my bedroom window when I am dressing in the morning, and my only garden seat is beside it, for relaxation when I return from the office in the evening. Once hidden by a tangle of willow and thorn, and segmented by banks and ditches, it is now a single stretch of water, broken only by three small islands.

4 *The Silver Garden* (0.25 acre)

Named after its collection of silver birches which stand out as a pleasant contrast against the darkness of the Spruce Grove, it was originally the site of the settling pans for the clay slurry. It is particularly liked by a wide assortment of vetches and fungi.

5 *Nut Glade* (0.1 acre)

This small glade merges the semi-formality of the Back Lawn with the wilderness of the woodland. Needless to say, it is planted with nut bushes.

6 *The Pinetum* (0.4 acre)

This is a rather grandiose name for a collection of ailing conifers. A ride bisects it: to the south I have left it in its original state, with a thick tangle of privet and elder to act as a bird sanctuary, the northern half has been cleared of undergrowth.

7 *The Mangrove Swamp* (0.6 acre)

Also rather an affected name, but it gives a good impression of the still, shallow expanse of water and the trees which grow out of it. Its waters curl round the mound of a pug-mill and broaden out again to form the Black Pool, near the grave of Wilbur, our pet pig.

8 *The Pasture* (1.5 acres)

Originally taken from a field to the east, ponies have now crept their insidious way into it. It has also proved a good launching site for hot-air balloons.

9 *The Spruce Grove* (0.2 acre)

Spruce does not like our cold, heavy clay and prefers acid to alkaline soil. The sullen trees in this forty-year old grove are half the size they should be, but are still tall and dense enough to kill off most of the undergrowth.

10 *The Larch Grove* (0.15 acre)

Like the spruce, the larch is not particularly fond of our part of Britain, but in this case the enemies are windblast and pine moth. However, the light shade gives a much wider and more varied undergrowth and Rosie, our donkey, found that the grazing there was the most interesting of all.

11 *The End Ponds* (0.75 acre)

Originally they were overcast by living trees and clogged with dead ones. Now cleared, herons and kingfishers are welcome visitors who do a good job culling the overcrowded fish. There are several ponds, the largest, the Far Pond, being about a quarter of an acre.

12 *The Beak* (0.6 acre)

I reclaimed this strip of land from a tenant farmer, firstly to rescue an old hedge from his plough and thus save the nesting sites of many wild birds (and less-wild game birds), and secondly to plant trees

Side view of House

on a ridge of land which can be seen over an area of about five square miles.

13 *The Orchid Glade* (0.4 acre)

Botanically, the most interesting part of the garden. It contains three different types of wild orchid and a large variety of grass and sedge. It takes almost as long to keep it "wild" as it does to keep the Formal Garden "tame".

14 *The Willow Carr* (0.5 acre)

An untouched swamp, mainly overgrown with willow and dogwood. A very good nesting site for birds of many kinds.

15 *The Orchard* (0.2 acre)

Fruit trees, mainly plums, were planted here as a more attractive substitute for the original brambles, thorn and elder. It is kept semi-wild in order not to look out of place, and also because I have given up the battle with bullfinches and other pests.

Amongst other features are the house itself with its adjoining out-buildings which include stables, a cart-lodge and the Pepperpot (an octagonal room next to the swimming pool); a large shed in the middle of the woodland known as the Pheasantry; the main foot-path, which leads from Nut Grove to Far Pond, and which is known as Gnat Walk; three circular mounds which are the remains of pug-mills or brick kilns; "Walt Disney's Oaks", a rather infantile name for a gnarled clump of pollarded oaks which look like a Hollywood setting for squirrels, rabbits, gnomes and other vermin; and the Blue Garden, around the swimming pool.

Although the house was given to me as a wedding present from my father, Dominie and I had a variety of other homes for the first four years of our married life. A newspaper, writing about our wedding in the sycophantic yet slightly snide tones used by gossip columnists, having described in glowing terms the famous or notorious guests, the size of the cake, the possible amount of money involved and the honeymoon in Madeira, ended tersely, "the couple will live in a bungalow in Birmingham".

In fact it was a bungalow near Derby. We rented it from a man who had thoughtlessly built it in a fog-pocket so that the curious eyes of neighbours were baffled by the thin mist which hung around for days on end, and by the frost-filmed windows which necessitated the use of electric light during much of the day. However, it was our first home and we doted on it. We were in that early stage of marriage when all one's actions seem to be part of a play entitled "Being Grown-Up". Dominie learned how to boil eggs and grill chops, I spent hours pruning both the rose bushes and cutting the tiny lawn with hedge clippers. I was introduced to the television – my father had thought it was an iniquitous machine craftily invented to dull people's minds – and I would stare at it in fascination, even at programmes like *Come Dancing* and *Blue Peter*.

Coronation Street became less of a programme and more a way of life in our next move, to lodgings in a terrace of houses in Liverpool. The house was two-up-and-two-down and was owned by Mrs Haltwhistle, a kindly soul whose most noticeable garments were tiny cardigans and vast slippers. When we arrived, she took us up to the bedroom and opened its door with a flourish and we were all disconcerted to see, lying on the huge bed which took up three-quarters of the space, the plaster from the ceiling.

I found the bathroom to be the most depressing of the amenities. We were expected to bath only once a week – Mrs Haltwhistle provided a packet of Daz for this ritual – and when I lay in the water I could hear our neighbour performing his most intimate and intricate ablutions and I could see spiders peering back at me from cracks in the walls. I am not over fastidious – no one who has done National Service could be – but one thing I could not abide was the thought of sharing the bath with the plug chain. This was so matted with decades of accumulated hair that it looked like a monstrous caterpillar creeping from the outflow, so before my first bath I set the whole thing alight. Poor Mrs Haltwhistle spent hours looking for an ember she thought was burning through the horse hairs of her sofa.

Mrs Haltwhistle was a hospital cleaner and spent all day out of the house. I was learning to weave and spin in a local mill, and every lunchtime I would walk back home in my overalls and have lunch cooked by Dominie. However for the evening meal, high tea, Mrs Haltwhistle would warm up the hospital food she had smuggled out in kilner jars; like all such food it seemed to be either mince or watery stew, stewed prunes and custard, or those lumps of sweetened dough whose names, dependent on size and shape, are either "Dead Men's Arms", "Dead Men's Legs" or "Babies' Brains".

Mrs Haltwhistle's nightly ritual still remains vividly in my mind. "Ah well," she'd say, "time for bed." She'd stand up, wade into her floppy slippers and then, with her teeth gritted and her screwed-up face puce with concentration and effort, she'd button up her cardigan over her colossal bust. Each button needed to be heaved towards its appropriate hole, and when the whole process had been silently completed, she'd gasp out in relaxation, stretching the row of circular gaps between each button almost to bursting point.

Our three months in Liverpool taught much to Dominie and me. We learned that poverty does not necessarily destroy pride, that a bad education when young does not mean that the old have not learned much, and that the community spirit in a row of dingy houses can be stronger and less selfish than it is in many villages. But it also showed us how boringly constricting life in a town can be: almost all that one did had to be planned or controlled by someone else and was organised for the crowd rather than for the individual. Most contact with nature was lost except for the sight of the sky and the snow, and both of these were often grey with pollution.

We moved next into one of the oldest houses in the north of England. Although it had been built around the year 800, it had been renovated in 1137 and thus had full medieval cons such as windows and an indoor staircase. The shepherd-monks of Fountains Abbey used it as a rest house for nearly four centuries, and I suspect that it was then that the central heating was installed: a rickety boiler which ate vast amounts of coke and just managed to stop the water freezing in the cast-iron radiators.

When Dominie and I lay in bed on lazy weekend mornings we could hear the warbling of the curlews and the bleating of the sheep on the moor, and through the tracery-headed Gothic windows we could see the tops of swaying trees in the garden burdened with rooks' nests; yet when we went through the door of our garden wall and walked thirty paces up a little "fold" between two old stone buildings, one a pub and the other a clothes shop, we were in the cobbled square in the centre of the village.

With the house, which we rented for £3 a week, went four acres of garden, the "gates" of 21 sheep on the moor, the right to hold a feast for the whole week following Michaelmas and the right to dig peat on the moor.

I left most of the gardening to old Tod Morden, the gardener, and concentrated on digging peat. This became an obsession. The topmost layer of any peat moor is fibrous, full of heather roots and tough, but after a foot or so it turns to the consistency of fruit cake and, if it is suitably damp, the spade slides in with little effort. Further down, ten feet or more, the peat turns a bluish-grey and is as easy as butter to dig into – but much heavier. I do not know how old the peat was at that depth, but the flora was different from that of the present, because it included silver birch and hazel. The remains of this scrub had the same soft consistency as the surrounding peat, but it was in such perfect condition that one could see the medullary rays in the wood and insect holes in the bark; after drying, these branches contorted, blackened and shrank. I was always in the morbid hope of digging up a coffin containing the perfectly pre-served remains of a bronze-age man, as they occasionally do in the Danish peat bogs.

In the autumn, Dominie and I would take the turves in carloads back home, and we would build a large stack beside the back door. I did not really want to burn the peat, it gave off no heat in our huge stone fireplaces, smelt of burning nappies, and it was a continuous source of pique to see my stack dwindle in size each day.

Morden thought peat digging a waste of time. He was a hand-some old man, invariably wearing a tatty army great-coat, and with a drip at the end of his nose. He had three obsessions: the central heating, the pigeons in the kitchen garden and the production of cabbages. All day one could hear his muttered curses about the first two, and every other day he would come into the kitchen bearing colossal cabbages with leaves like thick green linoleum.

Mrs Morden helped Dominie to do the housework. She was a sweet round little person, but always pointed out, with an air of despondent resignation, that she had married beneath her. She was therefore exceedingly miffed one day when her husband received the following letter from a famous Grammar School:

Dear Mr Morden,
    We are celebrating the four hundredth centenary of our school. We were founded in the sixteenth century by a Dean of Saint Paul's. We learn that you and your son are his last living

descendants and we enclose, for your interest, a copy of your family tree going back to the fifteenth century, a drawing of your coat-of-arms and crest; also an invitation for you and your family to attend our grand celebration feast.

When my job took me to London and I could then live in my own house by commuting to work – three hours per day – Dominie and I moved without much delight. We felt very much tied to the Yorkshire village where we had spent three happy years and had made so many friends, and we would miss the sleepy way of life, the moors and the rivers and the old stone house where George had been born; we were moving to a more crowded, busier land, and into a house that was ugly and cramped.

Just after we moved a great-aunt unfortunately died, but fortunately she left me her house, and with the money I got from selling it we enlarged Wastewood, and in this building Dominie and I, four children, six dogs, two cats and some uninvited mice live in permanent but happy bedlam.

Dominie is a red-haired Yorkshire girl and is the ruler of the household. She knows more about flowers than I do, particularly roses, and is basically responsible for the appearance of the herbaceous borders and the flower-beds, but she spends much of the time indoors scrubbing floors, washing clothes, cooking, looking after the children and doing the other things women like to do to fill in their spare time. She has started up a pony stud farm and Welsh Mountain Ponies now infest our meadows and whicker toothily from the barns and stables. Thus many of her appearances in the garden are whirlwind tours of advice and instructions, punctuated with pauses for picking, plucking, gathering and cutting, after which she disappears indoors: the little birds settle back in the bushes, the voles and mice creep out of the long grass and I continue the strenuous work of planning and meditating.

The children are Henrietta, George, Charlie and Candy: their ages range from ten to sixteen, but when we came here Henrietta was only three and George looked like a fat white maggot lying in a pram. The interest that the children have in gardening is limited to the burning of bonfires, the dredging-out of ponds and the use of the tractor-mower, but their presence can be discerned by an assortment of crudely made hovels amongst the trees, by the croquet and tennis balls which the lawnmower finds in the long grasses and by the rapid disappearance of hazel nuts and wild strawberries in the picking seasons.

Apart from the gardeners, whom I shall mention later, there are five other people of importance who affect our lives almost daily: a farm foreman, a gamekeeper, an estate carpenter, a scrap merchant and a neighbour.

The first three are employed by my father. The youngest is Tony Crisp, the farm foreman, he seems able to do anything from mending a chain-saw or re-fencing a paddock to driving a combine or planning a sales scheme for marketing Christmas trees. He does all this with a cheerful efficiency and determination which makes "Never-Sweat" Siskins, the village sloth and barrack-room lawyer, shake his head in melancholy disapproval.

Oscar Monk has one of those lined, weather-beaten faces which many gamekeepers have, possibly caused by the paradox of cosseting gamebirds for three-quarters of a year and supervising their slaughter for the remaining quarter. He is an encyclopaedia of knowledge on almost any subject, whether it be the Norwegian language or the migrating habits of golden plover, but is inclined to divide anything that moves into either "game" or "vermin".

Thomas Bradawl does all the odd jobs on the estate concerned with maintenance and repair; his skills are so versatile that he was able, with the help of three mates, to build the whole of Tony's house from foundation to roof ridge. His most noticeable feature is a large ginger wig which he wears for comfort rather than for appearance. This is disconcerting to those who do not know about it: on one famous occasion he used it as a method to speed up his shopping. He had been kept waiting in the builder's stores by a trio of dithering little old women who could not decide about the shape of some door knobs. Like most men under such conditions he kept sighing, raising his eyes up to heaven, wringing his hands and pacing about.

"Keep your hair on, Tom," said the ironmonger, finally irked by this fidgety pantomime.

He could not resist this hell-sent opportunity.

"No I shan't," he snarled, and whipping off his wig he slammed it on the counter.

The little old ladies gave out one united shriek, and having shruk, quit.

Michael Ryan lives amid his scrap heap at the end of our lane; as well as being an eyesore it is not even an interesting scrap heap being composed of old 'fridges and washing machines, rusting metal drums and corrugated iron, the whole lot in a tangle of rotting cars and vans which look like the discarded cases of dead insects. With his wild hair, bristly face and stocky form he looks, to Candy, like Mr Fuzzypeg the hedgehog, but a pair of amused, shrewd eyes belie the general innocence of his appearance. He spends much time in our kitchen, talking horses and swilling tea.

Finally, as a regular source of advice, help and friendship, we have our neighbour of five minutes walk away, Mrs Rutland. Her husband is a great friend of my father's, and like all that generation seems to have had a life which has been more active than those of a dozen people of my own age: he has been a professional poker player in the Argentine, a breeder of polo ponies and of pigs, a bookie, a circus rider, a rear-gunner in a bomber and a courier carrying explosives for MI6. He is now old and his mind drifts in a vast sea of memories; Mrs Rutland is as brisk as ever, looks after a large garden almost single-handed, and is a constant supply of help and of plants.

I thus set about my gardening not only with a spade and an axe, but also with a little experience and a lot of influence from family and friends.

CHAPTER 2

Tidying-up

"It's a bit of a puzzlement to know where to start," said Bell the woodman despondently, after our first tour of the grounds. There was only one part of the Formal Garden which was not overgrown or choked with weeds: the Rose Garden, a rather prim area of sixteen square beds surrounded by a thick, well-trimmed yew hedge. Most of the roses were as old as the house, forty years, and several needed to be removed; even the newer ones looked sickly, except for the Queen Elizabeth which had thrived into magnificence. As I have already said, our soil is good for roses: some of the woodland briars climb up twenty feet and have stems like long, thick, undulating snakes, and there are several excellent rose nurseries around Colchester which have sprouted on the rich clay, but, however good the soil, few bushes can easily tolerate a decade of neglect.

The rest of the Formal Garden was a rampant shambles. Most of the domesticated plants had lost the battle for survival to the natives. In the long herbaceous borders only three types of flower held out: a large clump of bergania pushed its thick shields against the surrounding blades of grass and ground elder; the occasional lupin could be seen lurking amongst the nettles and willow-weed, but these lupins had turned traitor by reverting to the pallid blue of their wild ancestors; Michaelmas daisies reared bright, defiant faces above the aggressive hordes of cow parsley and thistle.

The lawn, uncut for three years, was growing up to merge and entangle with the drooping branches of lilac; barberry and mock-orange had spread as an irregular fringe on to the weedy gravel

25

paths. The beech hedge along the lane towered more than fourteen feet, the laurel hedge in front of the house spread out dense, suckering branches and the yew hedge by the crescent border was bushy at the top with its spindly and scaly legs showing below, so that it looked like a row of ailing green ostriches.

Bell and I stared gloomily about.

"The lawn," I finally said, "it's the largest and most important part of the garden, once it's been cleared we'll have a better picture of what to do next."

All during that first weekend, therefore, I cut and hacked and mowed with an assortment of inefficient tools. An ancient scythe-mower did the first work: gnashing its jagged teeth through the long grass and also, as it was difficult to stop, through several small shrubs. After raking up the result of this primary effort, I went over the whole area with a small "Suffolk Punch", an extremely good little machine, but too small and exacting for the crude job I was giving it. It pottered about as well as it could but even with the blades set as high as possible some of the tussocks of cocksfoot grass were too tough and thick for it. These had to be cut with shears: had I known what a nuisance these invasive patches were to be in the future, I would have pulled or dug them out when they were still in tussock form. Finally, along the difficult undulating edges and the narrow strips of lawn which separated the rose beds, we used a small hand-mower, bought when I had become bored with cutting our billiard-table sized lawn in Derbyshire with hedge clippers; it had the maddening habit of getting jammed on even the minutest twig and of skidding ineffectively over any damp or mossy patch.

Rarely have I felt such overwhelming satisfaction from gardening as I did that Sunday evening, looking out of my bathroom window and seeing the neat stripes of green running in straight lines between the beds or curving artistically with the contours of the paths and bushes. The other features of the garden now stood out more clearly and pleasantly; it took a second glance to see that the hedges were still unclipped, that brambles were smothering the ornamental shrubs and the clumps of greenery in the beds were weeds.

While I was busy with the lawn, Bell attended to the paths and verges: trimming the edges of the latter and spreading sodium chloride on the former. By the following weekend the encroaching tide of green had turned brown and, in the weekend after that, I borrowed a flame-gun from my brother Sam and burnt up the dead herbage with a most satisfactory effect. A rain shower washed away the smuts and revealed the clean sweeps of gravel and the sharp, clean-cut edges of the verges.

Bell cheered up and decided that his offer to do some part-time gardening had been a good idea after all. He had been bored by retirement, well deserved after sixty years' hard work: his wife told me that he used to hone and polish his axe and rip every Monday morning and then hang them above the hearth with a melancholy sigh. He was unlike most of the locals, being dark, excitable and garrulous; and he gesticulated more than the average East Anglian, an unfortunate characteristic with him because one of his fingers, poisoned by blackthorn, had had its bone removed, and it used to loll and flop about over his hand in a manner horrible to behold. I have had two gardeners at Wastewood, first Joshua Bell and then, after his death, James Hart, and they both have had much in common: as well as being workers on the estate for all of their lives, they had developed great skill with their implements, Bell with the hook and rip of the forester, Hart with the scythe and pruning knife of the orchard keeper. Bell could cut hedges with his hook almost as quickly as I can with electric clippers and the completed work, even on a yew hedge, looked equally tidy; Hart can cut a lawn as closely and as evenly with his scythe ("Long Emma", he calls it) as he can with a lawn mower. Both of them were inordinately neat, anything that was not in a straight line or a perfect circle was an anathema to them. This was particularly disgruntling in spring when the snow-drops, crocuses and daffodils which I had asked them to plant at random sprouted in tidy formations as if they were Trooping the Colour.

It has always been my policy that, when possible, an expert be used for any job, whether he be a Chartered Accountant, marketing manager or gardener. One can then have an idea and start some-thing up – be an entrepreneur – and then hand over the details and the skill to the men who really know the subject. Both my gardeners have been more experienced than I, and I have felt no shame in listening to their expert opinions and in leaving them with the complicated work, whilst I concentrated on the menial tasks of digging, hewing and shifting earth. Sometimes I doubted their reasoning: Bell was convinced that his nose would bleed if he smelt a poppy, Hart thinks that things are better planted during the waxing of the moon and he cures his sore feet by putting gin and pepper in his boots, but their mixture of lore and science has often proved correct.

After the lawns had been mown, the paths cleared and all edging trimmed, Bell and I could see that there was still one basic task to be done on the general "bones" of the garden before the more complicated and fiddly work began: the hedging. This consisted of about a hundred yards running alongside the lane, the part opposite the house being of laurel, the rest of beech, and the yew which bounded the Crescent bed. We agreed that the difficult and meticulous work would be with the yew, and therefore Bell set to work on that whilst I dealt with the other. Bell's job was not arduous, but it needed a true eye: he had to cut the growth down to chest-height, this was done with a hook and pruning saw, and he then had to narrow the hedge by trimming off the irregular tufts of horizontal branches, this he did with his hook and rip. It was extraordinary how he managed to slice such even lines without a measure for the whole forty-yard length of the hedge, but although it looked immaculate from afar, on a closer look it seemed appalling: more than half the leaves had gone, the top of the hedge was completely open and showed the rows of circular stumps left by the saw, and the legginess of the base seemed even worse now that there were no overhanging branches left to cover it. However, within six months most of the hedge-side had changed into a smooth green wall, though it took a further two years before the top and bottom had completely covered over. We made one mistake in theory, but in practice there have been no bad effects; this was to cut the sides of the hedges vertically. Apparently the sides of a hedge should slope inwardly towards the top so that light can get to the lower leaves, but in fact all my hedges have perpendicular sides and they grow evenly and thickly right down to the ground. One place only is an exception, a particular length where Potter, my black labrador, scratches himself alongside the hedge, breaking off all the leaf buds and creating a bare, twiggy strip about twelve feet long.

In spite of having so much yew hedging, in principle I am not very fond of it as it is dark, poisonous and unattractive to most birds for nesting, but it is by far the best windbreak for any flowers which need protection. Holly or box are good alternatives, but take many years to grow and are expensive to buy. My other evergreen, laurel, I think most pleasant, but many people associate laurel with the dank clumps once seen in suburban rectories, the leaves darkened with soot or pimpled with variegated speckles and blotches. My laurel, Prunus Magnoliaefolia, has large polished leaves of a rich emerald green, the flower spikes are like small scented candles and it is always alive with birds, nesting in the spring and summer, hiding from the weather in the autumn and winter. In addition, according to Robert Graves, one can chew the leaves and get mythological hallucinations – presuming that one does not die first, which is more likely.

I still remember the strong and varying emotions I had as a small boy collecting butterflies: the delirious excitement when I caught one, the meticulous apprehension when I transferred it from the net to the killing bottle, the horrified guilt as the fumes from the crushed laurel leaves sent it to a fluttering death, and the pride as I surveyed the beautiful rows of corpses in my collection chest.

My beech hedge is almost as useful as an evergreen because it keeps its dead leaves on during winter, but I do not really like forcing a plant to be a short bush when it actually wants to be a large tree; similarly, while I admire the ingenuity and artistry of those who practice Bonsai, the tortured writhing of their stunted trunks and wizened arms gives me the willies.

On the western edge of the garden, along the ditch which separates the neighbour's field from the Back Lawn, I have tried a different sort of hedge, the spreading thicket. My attempts have not been very successful so far, mainly because of a collection of mistakes. The history of my gardening is a catalogue of errors: most of these being caused by ignorance, such as the time I planted a lime-hating Taxodium in the Mangrove Swamp; some being caused by a mixture of laziness and crass optimism, as when I strolled through the Larch Grove blithely sprinkling out packets containing fern seed on to the ground; some being a lack of planning, as when I had to move a six-ton heap of earth twice. My mistakes with this hedge were mainly the mistakes of crass optimism.

The line of hedge here is very old. You can often tell the age of a hedge by counting as centuries the number of woody species every thirty yards. Thus this hedge, which has at least one oak, maple, elm, hazel, sloe and hawthorn every thirty paces, is probably six hundred years old. This is likely, as the western edge of my garden is also the parish boundary, and these boundaries mark some of the oldest hedges in the country, many of the others being planted in the eighteenth and nineteenth centuries as a result of the Acts of Enclosure. (Incidentally, the tree-per-thirty-yard method of dating is liable to error: in some soils only a limited number of species may grow, or one type, such as elm, may crowd out the others.)

This hedge has not been laid for at least sixty years and so it now consists of a line of thin trees and scrawny bushes. The prevailing westerly wind sweeps through it with little hindrance and also one can see the walls of the neighbouring town, half a mile away. In order to plug these windy and visual gaps I first tried a rambling rose. The advertisement in a gardening magazine said that I would instantly have a thick, spreading hedge, full of scarlet flowers in the summer, and glowing with ruby hips in the autumn. This advertisement promised that each plant would be at least eighteen inches high, and I was therefore rather surprised when the ten dozen I ordered arrived in two shoeboxes. I was doubtful if the bunches of brittle twigs would grow at all: perhaps I was wrong, and perhaps if I had planted them with more care and less surly pique, I would now have the advertised "star-spangled" hedge. My next efforts in plugging the gaps were with bamboo. I sometimes get all of a tizzment over a money-making scheme: fish-farming carp for Japanese restaurants, growing teazles for the woollen trade, or buying old sailing ships in the Black Sea to charter off Colne Point; most of these ideas fizzle out as the experts tell me that they are either risky, expensive or plainly stupid. One of these schemes resulted from an article I read which said that about £3,000,000 worth of bamboo is imported into this country every year. In most of the local gardens bamboo, once planted, spreads like a weed, and it occurred to me that the stuff could be grown commercially. I eventually discovered that it had been tried before, unsuccessfully, during the war. It was found that the best place to grow bamboo was in wet and warm Cornwall, but even there it did not ripen into the hard, thick-stemmed canes wanted by the trade.

Whilst I was investigating all this, I learned to look at bamboo in a new light, and instead of thinking of it as boring clumps of rat-infested, overgrown grass, I began to appreciate the grace and variety of the species. A particular virtue of bamboo is the sound it makes. I believe some blind people can distinguish trees by their noise in the wind: the roar of an oak forest in comparison to the seething hiss of a spruce spinney, the whirr of aspen leaves compared to the murmur of a mulberry, the warm rustle of spring in comparison to the dry sigh of autumn. Outside my bedroom window, when I was a boy, there was an avenue of Lombardy poplars which my father planted. People said that he had planted so many poplars over the estate to please my mother, who is French; I was rather disillusioned when he told me it was to delude the tenant farmers: as the branches did not hang over the fields they made no complaint, little realising that their immense root system does far more damage to the crops than does the shade of oak or elm. All during my childhood, when I lay in bed, I could hear the poplars whispering outside my window; I now find it very difficult and unpleasant to sleep out of earshot of a tree.

Bamboos are quieter than trees, but they have a greater variety of sound: the leaves rustle and rattle, the stems clatter together, and they have, like the aspen, the uncanny habit of suddenly springing to life for no apparent reason.

I can understand the superstitious awe that man has had for the aspen. I remember standing by the Far Pond watching a pair of mallard, their family of ducklings like swimming bumble-bees. The air was absolutely still, gnats floated over the placid water and the fronds of the weeping willow hung limply in the sun. Suddenly, on the bank opposite, an aspen shivered into life, its leaves quaking for no reason that I could see, and my hackles crawled with primitive dread.

Fired with enthusiasm for the bamboos, I dug up my only clump, divided it up into a dozen pieces and transplanted them alongside the ditch, below the trees. Most of them died. The problem was water. One is inclined to think that the bank above a ditch, river or pond is bound to be damp, in fact it is much more likely to have better drainage, and thus be drier, than the land further from the water, and it is only when the roots reach the water-level that the plants begin to prosper. The three remaining clumps of bamboos are now beginning to spread, in a slow and unenthusiastic manner.

My last efforts to make a thicket hedge have been with snow-berry and Cotoneaster Simonii. These grow rampantly through the woods where Monk, the gamekeeper, planted them as a covert and a food supply for his pheasants. I took a large amount of rooted suckers, stuck them in the ground, watered them often, and was quite satisfied when about half of them struck: a reasonable thicket should now exist in five years. The white snowballs are attractive in winter, which compensates for the dullness of the small, pink flowers in spring; the Cotoneaster has bright red berries which match the scarlet autumn leaves; both species have a thick growth of suckering stems which is dense enough to act as a windbreak: in certain ways it is even better than a solid barrier, as it acts more as a filter and thus cuts down the turbulence which can be caused on the leeward side of a wall or yew hedge.

I have laid one hedge, the one running for 180 yards alongside the drive which leads to the Pheasantry. It had become tall and straggly, with ash stems shooting through it, starving the quickthorn roots of food and the leaves of light. Hedge-laying is a much more difficult job than it looks. Each part of the country has its own method, and it seems to me that it is in the East Midlands, especially around Rutland and Leicestershire, where the best laid hedges are seen. Perhaps this is because of the needs of the hunting landowners and farmers. When laying a hedge, almost as important as the bill-book and axe are the gloves: the only really suitable ones I found were army wire-laying gloves, made of heavy leather and armoured with rows of broad metal staples. I started badly, with the normal amateur's fault of cutting the hedge too high up: Bell showed me that the stems should be cut almost at ground-level and then woven into the already-laid, preceding sections; I did not bother to bind the top with hazel, as he suggested, as I did not mind if it was not cattle-proof.

I wish, though, that it were rabbit proof, for rabbits infest the whole garden, and my feeling towards them is similar to that of a restaurant next to a cinema showing *Watership Down*: its placard said –

"You've read the book
   You've seen the film
   Now try the pie."

A rabbit eats about 400 lbs of food a year; Monk says that eight rabbits eat as much as one sheep. They are thus highly unwelcome to gardeners and farmers, though since I have discovered the rabbit-proof plastic spirals for young trees, I get less agitated about their presence.

I once saw a "King" rabbit. We have plenty of "Parsons", a nearby wood has been known over decades for its colony of black rabbits, but I had never heard of a King until last year, when a small ginger rabbit scuttled from a pony pasture into the ditch. "A King,"

ACH.

Rose Garden before tidying

sighed Monk gloomily, "that means there is going to be an increase
in the rabbit numbers; whenever the wild rabbits start breeding
funny colours you know it means that we are in for a population
explosion."

"Parsons" are so called, one presumes, because they wear black,
but the only red-headed kings I remember are William Rufus and
Henry VIII. Ginger, although rare in some wild animals, is not
unknown: I once caught a ginger mole.

Although I have no love for rabbits, hares are different. The doe
drops its leverets in forms scattered in the long grass and visits them
on a routine tour to give suck. Potter met one of these lonely
looking infants in the Rose Garden, picked it up in his vast jaws and
dropped it, unharmed, at my feet. We presumed that the mother
would never accept a child with such a strong scent of dog, so
Dominie decided to rear it instead. Emily was utterly enchanting.
She became completely tame within two hours, after her first feed,
through an eye-dropper, of baby's tinned milk. (Monk told
Dominie that hare's milk is very strong, so cow's milk would be too
insipid.) She would hop solemnly up to every living thing she saw
and peer earnestly at it. Buzz's ill-tempered snarls as she tickled him
awake, or Algy's mean little eyes deterred her not one bit. She
embarrassed Potter terribly by adopting him as a foster-father.
Every time he lay in front of the drawing-room fire she would
hastily hoppity-hop across the carpet and snuggle down next to
him. He would then lift his great old head and stare beseechingly at
me, with the same expression my parents' chauffeur used to have
when my mother asked him to take Hercules, her minute Norwich
terrier, for his London walkies.

Grant, the chauffeur, was a large, red-faced squarely-built man;
he had a normally cheerful disposition, but he could not abide the
humiliatingly effeminate occupation of traipsing through the
streets of Belgravia in company with a pampered pet. His abhor-
rence for this pastime was increased one shy-making evening when
he met Mrs Moosa, the housekeeper from the embassy next door,
out walking with Fatima, her corgi bitch. Mrs Moosa and Grant fell
a-talking. Noting the quizzical expressions or raised eyebrows of
the passers-by, Grant eventually looked down and was disconcerted to see that he had, on the end of his lead, not one dog, but
two. Aghast, he hastily towed them into the privacy of the nearest
porch and tried to wrench them apart. Grant and Mrs Moosa

tugged and prised with no avail for half an hour in sullen but determined silence. When the nuptials were finally consummated his mortification was hardly diminished by Hercules' eccentric gait as they proceeded home: as if in memory of his recent pleasures the dog kept skipping and hunching along the pavement like a demented pop-singer.

I have sometimes managed to call some of the rabbits to me. One of my childhood heroes was a certain Dr Doolittle who could talk to animals, not only to his pig, Gub-Gub, and his parrot, Polynesia, but also to quite uncommunicative creatures such as snails and worms. Until I was taught by Monk, my nearest success in conversing with animals was by means of a weird little object which I bought through an advertisement in a comic. It was basically a wooden tube, into which was fitted a pewter plug. This, when turned, produced a chorus of squeaks and twitters, a cacophony which was meant to attract birds; unfortunately it was more effective in attracting other small boys who, intrigued by the sight of one of their fellows poised in the manner of a wine-waiter dealing with a stubborn cork, and emitting chirrups while doing so, would creep up to investigate: I would hear a rustle in a nearby bush, look up from my exertions over the "Audubon Bird Call" hoping to see a feathered friend and would meet, instead, the wondering gaze of Toadwell, McWhirtle or Ahmed Minor.

Monk had been brought up in the wild-fowling areas of the Lincolnshire Fens, and it was extraordinary to see how effective he could be in attracting most water-fowl with their calls: we would lurk in the narrow creeks of the saltings near Mersea Island, with the cold, grey sunrise shining on the wet mud and the chilblained fingers of the samphire (Glasswort) trembling in the cold east wind, and a skein would fly across the faded sky; instantly Monk would erupt into the appropriate honks, cackles, quacks or whistles, the skein would swing round towards us, and yet more unfortunates would be added to the pot.

The easiest bird to call is the curlew: they are so curious that they can be attracted by tufts of hay or leaves thrown into the air, or they will follow a dog back to the hide of its master. Once they were known as "the poor man's grouse", now they are protected which I think just as well, for they are better alive with their strange, evocative piping, than dead in a roasting pan.

Rabbits, too, are easy to call: all one has to do is to kiss the palm of one's hand in a noisy, drawn out manner – like the people one always finds oneself next to in the London underground – the resulting screech attracts rabbits who think it is one of their friends being killed by a stoat, and they can then be shot for their morbid curiosity. Morbidity can also attract crows and ravens: over the centuries they have learned that the clash of metal striking metal means a battle, and thus plenty of fresh meat, but motor cars have replaced the sword as the source of the noise, and the motorways are lined with sinister groups of waiting corvids.

During one's life, one gathers a few impressions, sudden pictures or visions, which return at occasions in a flash of vivid memory. One of my life-pictures is of a solitary figure on a lonely beach, singing to the sunset, her audience staring mutely at her from the cold Atlantic waves.

We were in the Orkneys, staying with Robert, my tree-hating friend whom I'll mention again later. As we walked along the rocky shore we noticed seals lying on the weed-fringed islets some hundred yards out. Robert told us that there is an Orkney legend that they are the souls of drowned sailors and if a woman sings to them they sometimes come to listen. We then, jokingly, suggested to Dominie that she tried, and after a few cries of modest dissent she walked on to the end of a spur of rock which jutted out into the waves, stretched out her arms and began to sing. The dying sun glowed through the wind-whirled tresses of her long dark red hair and she looked like some Celtic priestess keening to her sea-god.

A sleek, lead-grey head slid out of the water not far from her, then another, then several more until there were perhaps fifty or sixty silent, bland faces bobbing up and down with the waves, all staring at Dominie with round, wet, expressionless eyes like those of calculating corpses. Robert and I backed tactfully away, and as we did so the heads glided closer towards Dominie. Eventually, when some had come within a few feet of her, she suddenly found the whole thing rather ominous, stopped singing and turned towards us; within a moment all the little heads had disappeared below the waters.

If one remains still and wears clothes in greens and browns, one should be able to call many animals and birds, but I think that some of them can sense a killer: I remember walking through a wood with a cousin, in front of us Candy walked with one of her friends from school. The pigeons and rabbits let them pass, but as we approached them they vanished in a fluster of anxiety. My cousin and I had been brought up in the traditional British country way – if it doesn't move, prune it, if it does move, shoot it; the two little girls had never wanted to harm anything in their lives, and we wondered if the animals about us could subconsciously distinguish the killers from the innocents.

The only other sense I have noticed is the ability of pheasants to detect sound before it can be heard: sometimes, a few split seconds before a distant explosion (an artillery gun, an aeroplane breaking the sound barrier), the pheasants will call out; I suspect the noise might reach them as a quiver through the ground.

Old Mr Rutland is convinced that horses use their ears, like bats, to find their way about in the dark. When he was a gaucho in the Argentine he used to ride for mile after mile alongside the wire fences of the cattle stations. Much of this was done at night, but even on the darkest one the horses would not falter, but would canter on with their ears pricked well forward and the echo of their hooves bouncing off the hard ground and, he is convinced, off the fencing.

After the hedges had been dealt with, Bell and I took another walk around the garden. One of the nicest things about him was his enthusiasm, once he had been persuaded that an idea was a good one, he supported and elaborated this idea with suggestions and reminiscences. This was very different from Cyril, my father's former gardener, whose character can best be summarised by the following conversation that I overheard:

My father, pointing meaningly towards a weed, "Cyril, that is an extremely large thistle."

Cyril, with dejected agreement, " 'Tis, isn't it. It gives me a regular turn every time I see it."

Bell and I eventually decided that the most noticeable remaining eyesores were some ornamental shrubs, which either were being throttled by brambles and other growth, or were misshapen, or were too large and hiding views.

In front of the house the lawn was smothered with an assortment of bushes which had outgrown their welcome and were advancing in twiggy waves towards the building, blotting out the light and exuding a mouldy smell. Lilacs had suckered into large, non-flowering thickets, a huge broom had strewn the ground with dead branches, a heap of bramble, on closer inspection, turned out to be, originally, a mock-orange; amongst all this some half-dead barberries were grouped in unpleasing clumps.

I think some plants look unpleasant merely because they are uncomfortable to be among, otherwise, for example, the lush green leaves of the stinging-nettle would be attractive. Similarly, I have never liked plants which looked ill because of their colouring: the apoplectic purples of some copper beeches and Prunus, the leprous patches on the trunk of a plane, the mottled blotches of lungwort; on the other hand, this prejudice of mine may be considered inconsistent as I like yellow foliage, which to some people is anaemic. Most of the barberries combined the worst of all my dislikes, with puce leaves set about with bristling spines and shot through with lichen-covered dead twigs. Thus the smaller ones were razed to the ground by Bell's hook, and the larger ones were heaved out with a chain and tractor. I was interested to see that the splintered wood was a most vivid yellow. The only other wood I have seen of such brightness of colour was from a huge golden yew which was chopped down at my school in Morayshire. The heartwood was of a rich chestnut tinged with purple, and I spent much of

Rose garden after tidying.

a term sawing up slices and polishing them. Twenty-five years later I still have these slices and still have not decided what they can be used for.

Together with the barberry we cleared away the broom, mock-orange, some butcher's broom and a stump covered with honey-suckle – quite attractive, but messy and not comparable in magnificence to the waterfall of honeysuckle that covered part of the house and the garage twenty yards away. I was sorry about the broom, its trunk had a diameter of about 9 inches and the cascades of yellow flowers were superb; however, snow had broken many of its branches and its pleasantness in flower did not compensate for its ugliness during the rest of the year. I had wanted to keep the butcher's broom, botanically it is most interesting with its primitive flattened stems acting as leaves, but after I had cleared away the other shrubs it looked small and silly squatting amongst the surrounding trees. I replanted it in the edge of the woodland where it merges naturally into a thicket of wilder trees and shrubs. Monk says that it is like the elder and Lonicera Nitida in being disliked by rabbits.

After we had cleared this shrubbery there was a noticeable difference in the amount of light which came through the windows, not only because the sun was allowed to get in, but also because light was reflected off the paler surfaces of newly-exposed lawn rather than the murky surfaces of darker shrubbery. A further improvement was made when I had cut off all the lower branches of the remaining trees below 8 foot from the ground; this improved the view so that when one went up the short drive to the house it was possible to see clearly past the trunks to the lawn and rose-garden on the right, or to the broken-down shed, heap of coke-nuts and decaying hedge on the left.

Six of the remaining trees were laburnums, and I finally decided to keep them. I had been thinking of felling them because laburnum is so poisonous; the seeds, leaves and even the wood: dogs have died after chewing laburnum twigs. The very first thing that I had done in the garden when we moved in was to remove all the wild spindle berry growing near the house, I have heard that not only are its attractive triloballed berries very poisonous, but also there is no antidote for the poison. Later, I realised that the removal of all poisonous plants was a near impossibility; death-cap toadstools thrived on the lawn under trees, fly agaric (the red toadstools with white spots so beloved by Noddy and his mates) sprung beside the roots of silver birches, the berries of bryony and nightshade were looped like jet or coral necklaces amongst the thickets in autumn and, closer by, the fruit of the laurels and yew could tempt the children. I therefore spent much time lecturing them on the painful and fatal dangers of eating anything that was not actually given to them during meals and I emphasised this point, whenever I came upon the corpse of an animal or bird, by speculating that its death had been caused by disobeying its parents and eating something it shouldn't. I think the lesson sank home, because I used to hear Henrietta and George reproaching the corpse of some animal they were burying, with full and elaborate funerary rites, in the animals' graveyard under the drawing-room window. There are few things small children like better than a good funeral.

Of the other trees remaining in front of the house one in particular gave Dominie and me much pleasure. This is some kind of Malus – though that is a bit vague, as the family is connected to everything from pears and apples to medlars and roses. From its colouring and growth I think it is probably a Floribunda. In early spring, just when the first leaf buds are breaking and the tree is covered in a thin green haze, it suddenly explodes into such a mass of small flowers that the whole tree, branches, twigs and leaves, is completely enveloped in a billowing pink cloud. However, its main attraction to us was caused by the fact that we could see its top half as we lay in bed, and we could watch the masses of birds which loved, fought and fidgeted amongst its branches. There was the occasional blackbird or thrush, but mostly there were sparrows, a bird I have reservations about but which Dominie dotes upon. I like it for its friendly companionship as it nests in the clematis or as it hops after me as I am feeding the chickens, but it infuriates me when I see flocks gorging themselves on the newly-harvested corn, when I see the ragged remains of crocus and hibiscus, or when the scruffy bedding of a sparrow hangs over the edge of a swallow's nest.

However happy a marriage, there is bound to be the occasional disagreement, the first that I had with Dominie was over sparrows. We had come back from our honeymoon and were spending the weekend at my parents' house. As we wandered hand-in-hand through the garden we came upon a small wire cage.

"What's that?" asked Dominie.

"A sparrow trap," I said.

"A sparrow trap," she screamed, with the appalled surprise of someone who has discovered she has been nurturing a viper in her bosom; we then discussed it at length, Dominie taking the "sweet feathered friends" point of view whilst I tried to talk about vermin.

Country people often have an attitude towards animals which is incomprehensible to some people, particularly urban dwellers who cannot conceive how a man can call himself a lover of animals, and can certainly prove an interest, if not a love, by knowing more about animals, their names and habits, than can his critics, but who then follows his affectionate remarks by leaping on a horse and hounding a fox to its death. Perhaps this attitude can best be summarised by Mehalah, the wife of a warrener, who sometimes helps in the kitchen.

"As I was washing-up and looking through the window I saw two of the sweetest little rabbits playing together on the lawn; ever-so pretty they looked, and I said to myself, I said, 'What a pity Mr Courtauld isn't here with his gun!' "

It was now time to turn to the flower-beds. These consisted of:

1 A miserable, arid heap of soil under a row of alternate yews and bays which joinéd the lane to a broken-down shack (later replaced by the stables). Nothing seems to like growing under yew, and the only sign of green was a few sparse patches of dry, wiry grass, some brambles and goose-grass. I decided to clear the lot and gravel the area over so it could be used as an extra parking space.

2 The two beds running along the front of the house and separated by the front door. The right-hand one had been weeded by Henrietta and George to make their animals' cemetary and was covered with little crosses, most of which marked the successful attempts of Mildred and Tibbles, the cats. The other bed was occupied by a tangle of winter jasmine and clematis which had fallen off the walls and now coiled together amongst a clutter of dead leaves and old sparrows' nests.

3 A narrow bed running alongside the east wall of the house. As we were going to build the extension there, this bed was doomed.

4 The crescent bed backed by the yew hedge that Bell had just trimmed. It was entirely inhabited by ground elder.

5 The Rose Garden.

6 The herbaceous borders. They were both thirty-five yards long

and about fourteen feet wide. Bindweed and ground elder were the most prominent of the unwanted occupants.

Some anonymous ass introduced ground elder as a herb during medieval times. I have eaten it, mainly as an act of revenge, and it tastes of spinach mixed with iron filings. Bell told me that although one plant is capable of carpeting three square yards of ground in one year, nevertheless it is quite easy to get rid of, as the roots only go down to a depth of nine inches and therefore double-digging would do the trick. He and I accordingly double-dug, and as we advanced down the beds the ground elder sneakily appeared out of the soil behind us. Irked, Bell borrowed an old cultivator, and amidst clouds of fumes he minced the roots up into tiny pieces, and each tiny piece sent up its own tiny leaves. Infuriated, Bell set about with flame-throwers, poisons, hoes and blasphemy: the ground elder loved it.

We finally conquered this weed with what I consider to be my own contribution to garden techniques.

I originally got the idea when I saw the paint coming off my garage door. Tony Crisp had stacked a heap of his used broiler-house shavings against it. These soft-wood chips, impregnated with two months of chicken use, are full of nitrogen, potash and other goodies; they are also full of ammonia. If they are stored for a few months the ammonia loses its virulence, and the stuff becomes an excellent fertiliser and also lightens clay soils. When I saw that the pile of raw shavings, fresh from the broiler-house, had stripped off the paint from my garage door in two days, I thought it might do something equally as unpleasant to the ground elder; thus a thick blanket was spread over the beds. For two months not a weed appeared. I think the basic action was as follows: the ammonia scorched off all surface growth; the heat generated by the blanket caused rapid re-growth from roots and germination from seeds and this was either suffocated or, once again, scorched. After about nine weeks some leaves appeared, but very few and as they were easily seen amongst the grey-yellow background of shavings they could be hoed with ease. Thus I think that I have invented a combined weedkiller, fertiliser and soil-conditioner. It has one fault, it cannot be used around plants that are to be kept. The only ways of dealing with that problem, Mrs Rutland told me, is to paint the leaves of the weeds with a killer, and keep on doing it until they succumb, or to dig up the whole plant, clean the ground with a sieve, and replant after the roots have been washed clean. Bindweed, or "devil's guts", is slightly easier to deal with than ground elder, because although its roots can go down twenty-five feet, it also grows shoots which are long enough to put in a jam-jar of weedkiller; this must be boxed away from children and animals.

The Crescent border presented another problem with weed destruction, how to keep the weeds from encroaching from a nearby refuge. Once the broiler shavings had lost their potency, the embattled remnants of ground elder which had been skulking under the protection of the yew hedge began to steal out and re-invade their old territory. Persistent and tedious hoeing kept them just at bay but this seemed an occupation doomed to eventual failure. Finally I decided to make a grass path separating the hedge from the bed, using turves taken from the lawn on the site of the new extension; this path, regularly mown, acts as an effective barrier.

Whilst Bell was battling with the ground elder, I was transferring soil from the two unwanted beds to the rose garden. I had at first thought that these useless beds were barren of anything but weeds, but as I worked I noticed the occasional bulb, and next spring the rose beds were full of an extraordinary assortment of winter aconites, snowdrops, grape hyacinths, crocuses, narcissi and gladioli. Most of these were dug up later and replanted elsewhere, mainly in the Crescent border. The roses benefitted immensely from this fresh influx of soil, and have been magnificent ever since.

The beds in front of the house were a simpler problem: once the tangled creepers and dead leaves had been either removed, pruned or re-fixed to the wall, a quick going-over with a hoe was all that was necessary. My only problem was the edging. It had once been bordered by roof tiles, but these had all snapped, mainly at ground level, and the soil was spilling on to the drive. I took some big flints from the fields, but they looked untidy and inappropriate against the regular brickwork of the house. My next effort, larch poles, also looked out of place. I bought a strip of corrugated green plastic, but it looked extremely nasty and also it bulged unevenly under the weight of the earth. Eventually I used some of the bricks with which they were building the extension; these are made locally and blend with the other part of the house; thyme, aubretia and other low-creeping plants break up their formality and spread in pleasant cushions and shawls on to the gravel. The only material I really like is rock, when it is used locally, and it was one of the pleasures of

Yorkshire that one could just stroll out into the moor and pick up boulders or flagging for walling, paving and rockeries. In our part of Britain the only stone is flint, and the irregular shape of its nodules makes it difficult to work with.

The clematis and winter jasmine had been reinvigorated by the pruning and I had to decide quickly how to fix it to the walls. Hammering nails into walls does no good to a building, and so I discovered that living in a bogus Tudor house has one advantage, the use of the wooden beams for training creepers. I used brass hooks, but sparingly, so that Dominie would not notice their absence from her kitchen dresser. They were unpleasant to screw in, as the oak had become immensely hard, but once there, one can loop the main leaders over them and they never seem to fall off. It has worked particularly well along the main beam which runs for half the length of the house above the dining-room windows, the main stem of the Clematis Stellata which is supported by the hooks sends out streams of side shoots, and in the summer one can look out through a green cascade studded with white stars.

Unfortunately all this herbage becomes infested with the nit-ridden nests of sparrows. This horrifies Henrietta who is very fastidious, which is surprising, as her bedroom looks like an abandoned pig-sty taken over as a rubbish tip and then used by a dozen bankrupt dressmakers as their stock room. Her particular aversions are boiled fish, boys with spots, warm loo seats and insects. Great was her horror, therefore, when Mr Ryan told her that the martins' nests above her bedroom window and the sparrows' nests below it were likely to be full of bed-bugs. She now keeps her windows firmly shut, which adds to the general frowstyness of the atmosphere.

Our house has a large overhanging eave all about it, ideal for martins but never used before we moved in. Beneath it, I put one house-box facing west and two south. For three years they were ignored, but on the fourth spring several birds arrived. The first three families used the ready-made accommodation, two other families made their own. Luckily the eaves overhang enough to shade the nests; luckily also, the house-martins have not driven away the swallows as some people told me they would, but they keep apart, the martins to the garden sides of the house and the swallows amongst the open timbers of the outbuildings and stables to the west.

For many birds, natural conditions are not necessary: there are those birds which have taken over man's buildings either as an alternative to their natural home, such as the cliff-like walls and gables of houses replacing the rock habitats of martins and hawks; or the birds who like the by-products or protection of man, such as sparrows, herring gulls and swans; or the fools, who nest in car engines or letter boxes. The best example I have seen of this was when the Rutlands lived in an old manor house on the Essex marshes. Their drawing-room had a stable door leading to the garden, and the top half had to be left open all summer for the swallows who nested in the ceiling beams. Nothing worried these birds, and I remember when the Rutlands had a particularly noisy cocktail party; as the evening began each of the nests was edged with the rows of little black and white faces of the swallow parents and their broods, at the end of the evening, the swallows had showed their disgust with their uncouth neighbours by reversing, and each nest was fringed by a frill of little tails. One imagined that inside they had their wings over their ears.

As the garden developed and became neater some nesting areas disappeared; appendix B tells how I encouraged birds to stay in the garden, and which those birds were.

The Western Boundary Hedge

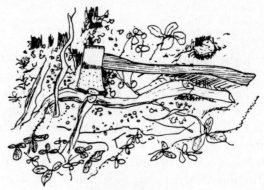

CHAPTER 3

Expansion – mainly the axe

Four months had passed. A regular routine of weeding, mowing and hedging kept Bell busy. Most of the flower-beds lay bare beneath their covering of broiler-house shavings.

I began to stray further into the wood. Much of this was impenetrable: dense, dark and thorny. The only path which existed was Monk's trackway, meandering from the back of the house to the End Ponds; skirting round thickets of thorn, angling off to the occasional glade where pheasant food was scattered and zig-zagging from warren to warren. I decided more paths were necessary; planning their routes was a specially enjoyable task. I classified my paths into two basic types, the first being chiefly used to get from one place to another, the second being used to dawdle, stare or brood; thus the former were reasonably straight and the latter veered from different points of interest.

To start, I decided to clear a path through the whole length of the garden, using Monk's track as a basis. I began by making a few changes in direction, partly to eliminate unnecessary detours and partly to thread the path through Larch Grove so that, for about thirty-five yards, one walked down an avenue of tall, straight boles. Most of the work involved the clearing of dead wood, scrawny trees or scrub, but stumps had to be cut to ground level and holes filled in to allow access for the tractor-mower. This machine cuts a three foot swathe, so one mowing up the path and one down it every other weekend has now resulted in a six foot wide alley of smooth, neat grass. Twice a year I cut an extra two yards on each side which keeps the taller weeds at bay, and the nettles and cow-parsley have given way to lesser but prettier flowers: bugle, ground ivy, primroses, violets and, near the Back Lawn where they do not look out of place, snowdrops. The path is roofed by the spreading branches of oak, hawthorn and one huge crab apple; from gaps between these trees shafts of light shine down and attract swarms of dancing insects. I like to see them; it was the children who named this path "Gnat Walk".

This main functional path changes, once it has reached the Far Pond, into the main meanderation which ambles back to the Formal Garden. It wanders between the ponds of Orchid Glade and then runs along the tops of the banks which bound the Willow Carr. Most of these were sharp-topped and narrow, so I dug away their pointed crests and used the surplus earth to widen them. The elevated causeway thus formed is entirely surrounded by water during the wettest part of spring. The route continues along the edge of Mangrove Swamp: the narrow strip of land between it and the hedge was widened for easier walking. Much earth moving was necessary along this stretch. I had to cart forty barrow-loads of soil to make a semi-circular detour round one old oak, for example. The path finally goes through the Pinetum and peters out on to the lawn by the Near Pond. I had originally presumed that this path would only be used by me during my rambles round the garden after my return from the office. But it is a bustle of activity. Dominie sometimes beetles up it to inspect the ducks on the Far Pond to see, as she puts it callously, "if they're fat enough yet"; Monk still does his routine visits, scattering wheat from a bucket and followed by the two boys who listen with respectful admiration as he points out the spoor marks of fox and wood mouse and tells them about his latest encounter with Pinkhorn the poacher; Henrietta comes home from school some weekends with a gaggle of friends; they drift up the path chattering in complete oblivion to their surroundings except for the occasional excited scream when they meet a nettle or spider's web; Candy solemnly takes me by the hand and leads me up the walk to her latest hut, where I have to pretend to eat her mud pies and moss puddings; Hart sallies out of his cottage on odd evenings and he and Florence, his mongrel, wander up to talk to his old friend Elijah Titmus who takes his grandson to fish in the Far Pond.

Thus the track is getting worn and I keep experimenting with different types of grass seed to see which can survive both the shade of the trees and the erosion of boots, shoes, sandals and paws.

The basic paths having been made in the woodland, two other things remained which made me feel restless: the scruffy shambles immediately behind the house, and the blank wall of elder which blocked the end of the walk between the herbaceous borders.

The area behind the house was extremely unattractive: parts of it showed the raised ridges of an old kitchen garden; in other areas sunken depressions marked the sites of extinct flower-beds; a broken-down shed and a large patch of nettles were the remains of a chicken run; various parts were bounded by collapsed wire netting festooned on rusting metal posts and with no evidence of what they had once contained. A few elders and clumps of bramble had sprouted at random but the site was clear enough to show the whole desolate scene in one glance, whilst other glances revealed old tins, broken bottles and an inordinate amount of rusting springs from beds and sofas.

I decided that the best thing to be done was to unite the whole hodge-podge into one lawn. I like wide open spaces in a garden and at that time mine consisted of a muddled complex of paths, small patches of lawn, lines of shrubbery and randomly spaced flower-beds. We also needed a reasonably sized area where the children could play without restraint: furthermore, as we were almost surrounded by trees, I wanted this fact to be emphasised by pushing out some space into the encroaching woodland so that a glade-like effect would result.

All inflammable rubbish, including the chicken shed and the cleared brushwood, was piled into a heap in the middle of the area. I am not good at judging heights, but I have one yardstick – if that is the correct word in this context – a double-decker bus is fourteen foot eight inches. This stack was about one bus high. It dominated the site which I had already begun to call, with gardener's optimism, the Back Lawn, for two months, then one evening I lit it and it changed into a most satisfactory inferno with flames and sparks which I judged to be at least four buses high. Next morning, when I looked out of my window, I could at last see in reality the general outline of the lawn-like glade which before I had only seen in imagination.

The next to go was all the metal and glass rubbish, this included the fencing and a wide variety of nails and iron-mongery raked out of the ashes of the bonfire. In all, I collected two cart-loads of junk which Tony Crisp and I took to Mr Ryan's scrap-yard.

He plodded out of his gate and gazed at my offering with disfavour.

"What do you want me to do with that lot?" he finally asked, after a chilly silence.

"I rather thought you might want to buy it," I replied wistfully.

He looked at me with a mixture of scorn and pique. "I'm a waste merchant, not a rubbish dump," he said, only half truthfully, "leave it in Witham Station, they'll never notice the difference."

I re-borrowed the scythe-mower from Sam to do the first cut on the Back Lawn, and above the clatter of the machine I could almost hear the wringing of his withers as he watched. Not all the bed-springs had been found and occasionally one would twang across the ground, having first left a shiny new notch in the scythe's teeth. I also met some stumps of the iron posts which had been snapped off at ground level during my efforts to remove them. Ground level they had been but once they had snapped they seemed to creep slowly out of the ground like the Young Maid of Hoy. I eventually had to dig them all up. What I took to be tussocks sometimes turned out to be ant-hills, and as the cutter munched its increasingly toothless way through them Sam's expression grew distinctly testy.

Additional problems were the irregularity of the ground, the sunken or elevated relics of former cultivation and also the holes and hillocks left by rabbits and moles.

The site was too large to make perfectly flat, besides, slight undulations gave it an added interest, but I intended to make it smooth. This was reasonably easy as building the house extension had created a large pile of superfluous earth removed from levelling and foundation work, this I wheelbarrowed to the appropriate places, dumped, raked flat and seeded. The moles were evicted by moth-balls and lengths of bramble being left in their runs, the rabbits were introduced to Monk's ferret.

I can still remember the first time I went ferreting, thirty years ago. Monk took me to a large warren in which all the burrows except two had been blocked. He put me beside one and told me to shoot any rabbit which came out, down the other he put a bad-tempered old dog ferret called Captain Farquharson. Occasionally we could hear a rumble deep underground as a rabbit ran from the

Gnat Walk from Nut Grove   D.C.H.

approaching terror, and my infant eyes popped with horror as I thought of the panic happening beneath my feet.

We waited. I riveted my gaze to the entrance of the burrow. My small ·410 grew heavier and heavier. My thumb became white and numb with the pressure I was putting on the safety catch. Suddenly there was a movement in the burrow. I whipped up the gun to my shoulder and fired.

"Good shot," said Monk bitterly, as he picked up the stone-dead Farquharson and chucked him into the ditch.

I know of two other people who have done exactly the same thing.

The Back Lawn was beginning to look like a lawn, albeit somewhat blotched with the marks of bonfires and newly-laid soil. Part of the expanse was interrupted by a line of fruit trees; these fruited well but they looked out of place and bisected the area. They had once been trained along a wire fence as cordons but having been untouched for several years now ranged in height from half to a whole bus. Most of them were unattractively shaped and, being too close together, grabbed and clawed at each other with contorted branches. After much brooding I decided to remove them all except the one furthest to the west, which was larger and better shaped than the others and could act as a well-placed specimen. Bell advised me not to fell them as the stumps would be a nuisance, but to pull them out with a tractor and chain. They were winkled out of the ground with pleasant ease; it was harder work filling in the holes and the tractor ruts with yet more carted soil.

From the house we could now see a clear expanse of lawn for seventy-five yards, right up to the towering line of Lombardy poplars. The lower boughs of the scraggy boundary hedge were lopped so that one could walk freely in the shade of the overhanging branches. To the east, the round clump of evergreens looked pleasantly cool with its dark shadows.

After two years of regular mowing much of the unwanted growth had vanished – brambles, nettles, docks, cow-parsley and hog-weed – but these have been replaced by sorrel, plantains, daisies, dandelion and clover. Several attempts were made with weedkiller, but it was a laborious, expensive and futile task. Finally, after Crisp had sprayed a pasture, he brought the tractor-borne crop-sprayer on to the lawn and gave it a going-over with the hormone killer. This was drastic treatment, but I had much pleasure a week later in gloating over the shrivelled corpses of my enemies; the grass, although scorched in a few patches, recovered after a few weeks. A few weeds have now returned, but I do not mind the occasional star of a daisy or blue sprinkle of speedwell so long as it is obvious that they are there as guests and not as aggressive squatters: I try to maintain a "controlled" ecology.

Ecology has recently become a source of particular interest to the general public. This science is concerned with the relationship that living elements have with each other and with their surroundings, with particular emphasis on the natural grouping together of various forms of life in different conditions. Although my particular patch is small, it is large enough to contain a good variety of conditions which have their own specialised communities of plant life. Land and water, light and shade, woodland and meadowland, all these are obvious comparisons, but in addition there are more subtle ones which need a second look before they can be discerned.

The Silver Garden is a good example. The basic conformation of this area can be described as open woodland, the very light shade being caused by the well-spaced and sparsely foliaged birches. The foundation is unique to the garden because the soil covering over the chalk is very thin, four to five inches; it is also well-drained. As a result it specialises in low-growing and shallow-rooted plants: amongst the short grasses grow violets, wood anemonies, bee orchids and primroses, a wide variety of vetches, centaury, hairy hypericum and strawberry – both the delicious edible kind and the frustrating barren strawberry whose fruits are little dry clumps of seeds. In general, the flora is similar to that of the Sussex Downs.

When standing in the middle of this particular community, one can see, close by, colonies of contrasting settlements: the space under the heavy shade of the oaks to the north is dominated by comfrey, nettles and some clumps of dogs mercury; wood false-brome, pendulous sedge and dewberry fill the moist, dark hollow by the Black Pond; on the sloping banks to the east, where I had put the soil excavated from the clay pans, the plants are taller and more luxuriant, with cocksfoot grass overtopped by a rapidly spreading growth of umbels such as cow parsley and hog-weed whose long parsnip like roots can drive deep into the soil.

Even a fairly small mound can show several ecological groups. The yard-high bank which I use as a footpath to skirt the Willow Carr has three different groups: wood sedge, primrose and dead nettle on its south-facing side, scarce sedge, bugle and ground ivy on its wetter and darker northern side, and moss and plantain on the beaten track on top.

Conditions in the garden are always changing, not only through my efforts with spade and axe, but also through natural processes: rampant growth begins to dominate the weaker neighbours with roots and shadows; grazing by rabbits – or ponies – can eliminate some types of plant and encourage others; even the steady drizzle of falling autumn leaves can enrich the land and encourage the growth of plants which, before, could not tolerate the soil. Thus, much of my time is spent in creating the right conditions for certain types of ecological communities and, having created them, struggling with Nature to keep the status quo.

When we stood by the front door and looked due east, the view ran in a straight line for eighty yards, firstly between the beds of the Rose Garden, then along the lawn walk between the herbaceous borders; it finally halted at a blank wall of scrub which marked the edge of the Pinetum. This scrub was dominated by elder, with privet, thorn and bramble as secondaries.

Elder is a most objectionable shrub. The smell of its crushed leaves is more repulsive to me than almost any other smell, except for the smells of decay. People make a sickly syrup out of it and whenever I win anything at the village fête it invariably turns out to be a bottle of this elderberry wine. It is extremely tenacious, and when cut down it behaves like the Hydra and sprouts even more heads: one of our woods was once infested by a huge murmuration of starlings for three winters, their guano killed several trees and all of the undergrowth, except for the elder, which thrived. However, I admit that the flowers and berries are pretty, and the plant is useful for keeping witches at bay – that is why so many old cottages have elder growing by their doors; elder wood should never be used as logs, for it was the timber from which the Cross was made.

The full-stop to the view was unsatisfactory. I wanted to see it continue right through the Pinetum up to the Pasture. Had I looked at a large-scale Ordnance Survey map, as I have done recently, I would have seen that this had once happened; as it was, I was suprised by the apparent fluke that there were no large trees in my way, and so with the use of long-handled shears, rip and axe, it took only two weekends to clear a green tunnel through the wood to the field beyond. My view from the front door now extended half a mile, over three fields to the roofs of my parents' house.

Although it opened up the view, this tunnel was somewhat dark and dank so I decided to clear the whole Pinetum by cutting the undergrowth down to waist level, and the lower branches of the trees up to twenty feet (the height that Bell and I could go without, as he said, "going all of a tremble".) I imagined that the effect would be like a green colonnaded tent, with birds gliding amongst the tree trunks between the two layers of growth; airy and mobile above, compact and even below. It took me five weekends to hack the northern half of the Pinetum scrub to a three-foot height, and another weekend up a ladder to saw off all the lower branches. By the time I had finished, the bushes I had begun with had already sprouted several inches, and had also grown out sideways so that it was almost impenetrable to anything but an elephant.

"I knew that would happen," said Bell with smug satisfaction, as I was looking crossly at the mass of new growth.

"Goddamnit, why didn't you tell me then?" I snapped.

"Because he knows you never listen," said Dominie coming up

to us and holding a steaming thrush's nest in her hand. "Who put this in my oven?"

I admitted sheepishly that it was George and I. We had found the abandoned nest and George, who had spent two weeks at play-school making a pottery worm had wondered if the mud lining of the nest could be baked into a pot.

"A rather silly idea," said Dominie in Joyce Grenfell-like tones, "please leave my oven alone, and clear up the mess you have made here, instead."

I decided to continue the work by razing all the undergrowth to the ground on the side I had dealt with, but leaving the southern half of the Pinetum untouched for the benefit of the birds and insects.

Elder is a soft and easy wood to chop down, but the privet had thicketed into sizeable clumps, with hard and thick stems in the centre and whippy outer suckers from which the axe rebounded. The random thorn and ash saplings added to the general problem and even with the tractor and chain it took six weekends before all the scrub had been cleared and was stacked in a huge pile on the dried-up bed of the Mangrove Swamp.

The rewards for all this effort are great, particularly in the morning when I am getting dressed at seven o'clock and looking out of my bedroom window. The rising sun sends beams of light shafting down between the tall trunks and dapples the ground below. Foxgloves have spread naturally, and the cyclamen I planted lie in pink drifts. The hollow, cathedral-like effect given by the arching roof and columns adds clarity to the songs of the blackbirds and thrushes which echo overhead.

The Near Pond is a long, irregularly shaped stretch of water about thirty yards north-east of the house. During our first year in Wastewood this was not a pond but a dry collection of pits with grass, sedge and willow-weed growing on the bottom, and thickly surrounded by scrub, much of this being thorn and willow. In our second year, to our delighted amazement, it filled with water. Being almost on the top of a plateau, the level of our ponds is affected by the water-table only: there are no springs. This results in fluctuating levels both seasonally and annually: the ponds are normally their deepest in spring, then they slowly seep away until by September or October several, particularly the shallow Man-grove Swamp, may be bone dry; the rains, which usually start on

November 5th, then gradually fill them up. If the annual rainfall has been particularly low they never fill at all, and in early spring the garden is full of frustrated amphibians looking for somewhere to breed. This varying water level does not affect the Far Pond so much; it is deeper and larger than the others and it is also fed by land drains from the adjacent fields.

I occasionally net some of the crucian carp which live in the Far Pond and distribute them amongst the other pools in the – perhaps naïve – hope that they will keep down the plagues of mosquitoes. These fish breed, and the resulting progeny have to be scooped up in shoals when the ponds dry out and returned to the Far Pond. Once I put fourteen goldfish in the Near Pond. Most of them were small, but they were old enough to breed and our children spent many ineffective hours fishing for the inch-long transparent fry. Goldfish do not get their colour for two or three years when in the wild, but they seem to be fertile at an early age, and when the pond began to dry I filled a rubber dinghy with water and put almost three hundred goldfish in it. This was in spite of the efficient angling which had been taking place by a family of kingfishers, a heron and our cat.

Kingfishers are meant to be shy birds, so we were very surprised and flattered when a pair took over a deserted rat hole just forty yards from the house. An old tree stump protruded from the water a few feet in front of their burrow, and this became their fishing platform. With their turquoise, blue and orange markings they looked extraordinarily exotic amidst the commonplace English vegetation, and when they flew within the dark recesses of the Mangrove Swamp they seemed more like flashing fireworks than like birds. I do not think that their eggs hatched for I never saw any young, and they have never nested here again, but we still see the occasional meteorite darting across the water as they make a foraging visit.

Another regular visitor is a heron. He normally keeps to the tranquillity of the End Ponds, but early in the mornings, as I stand by my bedroom window, I often see him peering at his reflection in the Near Pond. He is very nervy and if I twitch a curtain or button a shirt with too much of a flourish he lumbers into the air and sails over the Mangrove Swamp, his plumage merging like smoke with the silver-grey of the willow leaves. Some people worry about herons eating their goldfish, and put complicated bits of string or

The Back Law

netting below the surface of the water to keep them away. I have been told that they like to walk to the water's edge after they land, and a single strand of wire a foot high on the bank will deter them; perhaps they really are too stupid to think of stepping over it. Similarly, they do not like water too deep to stand in and as they will not catch fish swimming lower than their feet, they never fish from the bank. As my fish breed faster than the birds can eat them I let the heron bide.

My tolerance was different with the cat. We had rescued him from an excessively cruel and unpleasant man in Yorkshire who had left him to starve in his house, having first kicked him so hard that his head was like a white furry football with two bloodshot eyes and a swollen, protruding tongue. A little old woman came and asked us to look after him. Within three weeks he had grown fat, glossy and tame, and had eaten one of our budgerigars. The owner, on returning to the village, noticed this improvement and one day he knocked on our door and told me that he was pleased that we had the cat and that he reckoned that he was very valuable. I said that I was pleased that he was pleased and that we would take good care of it. After some other desultory talk he hinted that when he got annoyed he was rather inclined to hit people in their toffee-nosed faces. I replied that I found that most interesting because I had perfected, instead, a method of booting them in the crutch. We parted with mutual understanding, and the cat stayed with us.

Pooh, as we called the cat, turned out to be an immensely crass animal. He was large and white and fluffy, with an extra-baggy pair of trousers and a mane. He would stare at things with his huge yellow eyes and with an expression of astonished imbecility. He was very fond of the notion of climbing trees, and would frequently hurl himself at one, sometimes getting as high as six foot before sliding backwards with a screeching of ineffective claws. He was particularly affectionate when I was weeding, twining himself between my hands and the weeds and finally jumping on to my bent back, purring loudly, coiling round, and pretending to go to sleep.

He showed skill in only one thing: fishing. It took him a lot of practice, and we were puzzled by his frequent appearances in the house, soaking wet and mewing indignantly: but after a time, goldfish began to be found on the banks of the pond, invariably with long scratches down their sides. What annoyed me most was that they were always the largest and fattest of the fish. One day I found the cause: Pooh used to wait by the part of the pond which had a sloping and shallow bank, and when a fish drifted by he would scoop it out of the water in the same way I have seen televised bears catching salmon.

As I was saying, the Near Pond was dry our first year. We called it, in anticipation, the "Sunken Garden", envisaging a smooth lawn carpeting the floor and phlox, perrywinkles and pinks cascading colourfully down the banks; a rock-garden would be built in the steepest part of the banks and clumps of small alpines and ferns would replace the tangled dogwood and thorn.

Apart from a clear patch near the house, the whole area was surrounded by scrub. By now I had become fairly expert in clearing this type of growth, but the high, steep ridge of earth which separated the pond from the settling pans proved a more difficult problem as it carried oak, ash and thorn up to forty-five years old. Had I known that I was eventually going to dig away the whole earth-work, I would have pulled these trees out and thus loosened the soil and also saved an immense amount of tedium with roots. However, at that time, I envisaged it as a sort of elevated walk above the "Sunken Garden".

Eventually the area was cleared. The trunks and larger branches lay trimmed and neatly stacked in readiness for the circular saw. A colossal mound of brushwood rose from the centre of the hollow. A Guy Fawkes was hoisted upon it and for a week underwent more changes of clothing than a striptease dancer. On coming back from work on Monday evening, I found Guy Fawkes grinning smugly in an old torn jacket which my father had given me. It had been made twenty years before I was born. I took it off with cries of protective indignation. Next evening Fawkes was wearing my old school jersey which although worn at the elbows was very comfortable. During the following days he changed in and out of my trousers used for painting and creosoting barns, my mountain-rescue anorak, and a Girton gown for which I had a sentimental attachment. On the great day he was kitted out in a hideous rayon dressing-gown, a yellow tie with mauve horseshoes, given to me by a French aunt, my old rugger shirt and some heavy woollen army socks. He sat in these for the next three weeks while it poured with rain, and was finally executed in a smaller bonfire elsewhere as his original pyre was now standing in a foot of water; the water continued to rise and the burning of the stack took place two autumns later, when they had subsided once more.

Most of my bonfires were built over tree stumps in the hope that these would be burnt to ground level. This hope was usually unfulfilled: the heat from a fire seems to go up rather than down – in the colder days of Victorian England Londoners used to build bonfires on the frozen Thames – and only the dryest or most rotten stumps disappeared. Eventually I drilled holes in a few, filled them with salt-petre and set light to them, but even this did not work with most stumps. Then one day the boys and I went to inspect a charcoal kiln I had made. Because I had been lazy, and had merely covered the fire with wet leaves and blanket moss instead of turf, the fire had burnt out, my intended charcoal included, but so had the stump. I now use this method to get rid of any unwanted stumps or roots.

The front of the house became very constricted: our cars had to be parked outside after the garage was converted into stables; a large horse lorry was bought and took up more room; people would arrive in a variety of transport and park them in the tiny yard whilst they sat in the kitchen and talked over their tea: Monk with his Land-Rover, Tony with his tractor and Mr Ryan in a mobile scrap heap. After much wrangling and bargaining I therefore bought a fifth of an acre from the neighbour to the west. The scruffy hedge of bays and yews was bulldozed out and the resulting expanse was gravelled over; we then had a yard about 120 feet in diameter. Bradawl built a cart-lodge on the edge of this so that we could park the cars and Dominie's pony traps. The drive had had two entrances, I covered over one of these with the bulldozed soil and thus joined up the "D" shaped bit of front lawn with the rest of the Formal Garden. The remaining entrance was moved to the other side of a large oak which had originally marked our boundary, and the old gateway was filled in with the stumps of the removed bay trees. They hated the move, and have taken ten years to grow four feet high.

We do not go to the cinema much, perhaps a couple of times a year: one film we did see was *Doctor Zhivago*. I went with reluctance, suspecting the film would be as boring as the book, but I enjoyed it well enough and I was entranced by the scenery of the birch forests: the ghostly silver trunks dwindling into a pale green distance, the silence and the immensity. I decided to reproduce this – on a somewhat smaller scale. We already had the makings of a birch glade, for several of the trees that were growing amongst the scrub in the old settling pans were silver birch.

About this time we employed a new woodman. The estate had not had one since Bell had retired: for ten years the woods had grown unbrashed and neglected. My father and I decided that we could just afford a woodman, but more as a luxury than a necessity because, apart from a few specialised trees such as walnut and cricket-bat willow, trees do not grow economically in our low rainfall of less than twenty inches a year and it is a waste of money to go in for forestry on even a large scale. We chose Howard, a nice man with a wide knowledge and interest in the natural world; amongst the equipment we bought for him was a chain-saw.

Working with one of these was not as easy as I had supposed. We had found an old second-hand one; it was a brute to start, it weighed over a stone, and when it condescended to work it vibrated, roared and sent up huge clouds of blue smoke. The spinning fangs of these machines are wickedly dangerous, and the fact that I pour with sweat when I use one is due more to fear than to exertion. If used incorrectly, the branch or trunk being sawn can collapse on to the blade, causing the saw to shriek with anguish and shoot out sparks; one or two people have fallen on them with the most melancholy results; even worse, when felling trees, is the "bounce back", the branches of the falling tree act as springs and propel the sawn butt towards the feller. This once happened to one of Bell's mates.

"There was a great old 'thump' and there Fred lay, 20 feet away, with his broken leg sticking up like a tent pole. The rest of us couldn't help but laugh."

However, I finished in three weeks a job which would have taken fourteen had I used merely my axe and rip. The white trunks of twenty-three birches stood out clearly against the dark background of Spruce Grove. The birch is a most graceful tree and its long, thin twigs with their racemes of small leaves have a weeping effect as they stream down from their high crowns.

In removing all the undergrowth from the settling pans I had laid bare the straight division banks and ditches so instead of a romantic birch wood I had created something which looked like an abandoned sewage farm. This, and the fact that the "Sunken Garden" had become a group of ponds caused me to lay down my axe and reluctantly pick up my spade.

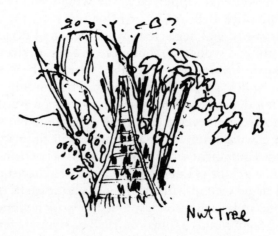

Nut Tree

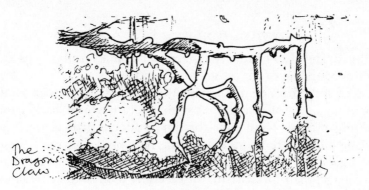

The
Dragons
Claw

CHAPTER 4

Landscaping – mainly the spade

It was not only the settling pans which showed their industrial origin, now that the Near Pond was full of water, its banks which had been cut by clay diggers were fully defined in their straight lines; neat ridges cut across the water and divided the hollow into small square or rectangular pools. My first priority was to create a single stretch of clear water, my second was to transform all straight lines and right-angled corners into curves to give a more natural appearance.

The primary work was fairly easy and extremely satisfactory. The soil consisted of two layers, heavy yellow clay for about two feet, and then chalk. The clay was immensely weighty, particularly as it was waterlogged, but it was almost as easy to dig into as had been the peat in Yorkshire. There were very few stones in it, and the roots were mainly of willow, usually thin and soft enough to sever with the spade. The chalk was harder and more compact, but was still soft enough to admit a sharpened blade with my fourteen stone of weight behind it. What was a nuisance, however, was the tenacity of the clay as it clung to the spade. It is extremely mortifying and frustrating to use all one's arm, shoulder and stomach muscles in an effort to fling a clod of clay into the distance, only to find it still squatting on the blade after the flurry of energy.

Then, for my thirty-fourth birthday, Dominie gave me a present which was to enhance my gardening in a dramatic manner: it was a stainless-steel spade with a ribbon on its handle. The ribbon was only there to soften the austerity of the present, and after it was removed, and after I had unwrapped some books from my parents, a rabbit made out of a lavatory roll from Henrietta, a curious lump of baked soil with a dent in it which George told me was an ashtray he had made, a toffee together with a penny from Charlie, some shooting mittens from my labrador, Potter, a trowel from Mrs Rutland and a note from Sam saying he would give me a present after I gave the one I owed to him, I hurried out to use the spade, more in tact than enthusiasm, for I secretly thought that a stainless-steel spade was like any other spade, but more shiny. I was wrong: the first clod that I dug went sailing off the blade like a curling stone on a sheet of ice, and I am sure that this spade has tripled my rate of work.

I find digging an engrossing occupation. When I was a child I was convinced that, if I had existed before, I had been either Julius Caesar, Alexander the Great or Francis Drake. However, I have met so many people who have also been these notables that I have now begun reluctantly to admit I was probably an obscure farm labourer, and that is why I have such a natural inclination to dig and delve. Henrietta tells me that it is because I am a Taurus, and all Taureans like messing about in mud. Perhaps I would not be so engrossed in this occupation if my livelihood depended on it; a pastime inevitably becomes a tedious chore if it is forced upon one. As it is, I find digging is like walking: it speeds the flow of blood through my brain and sends me into a busy trance full of day-dreams, plans and speculations.

Those who are scornful about manual work have the wrong idea about it. I remember being taken round the Ford factory in Dagenham with my platoon. We saw lines and lines of people standing by lines and lines of conveyors and doing the most incredibly dreary jobs. A guardsman asked one man how he could abide dropping bolts into iron plates all day.

"You see that clerk in that little glass office?" asked the workman. "He thinks he's better than me because he wears a suit and tie and doesn't dirty his hands. But he's got to waste his brain thinking about production rates and scribbling down columns of figures: but while my hands are doing this I can use my brain for anything I want."

I have marked on the map opposite the sequence of digging. Perhaps the most satisfactory was the very first object, the island

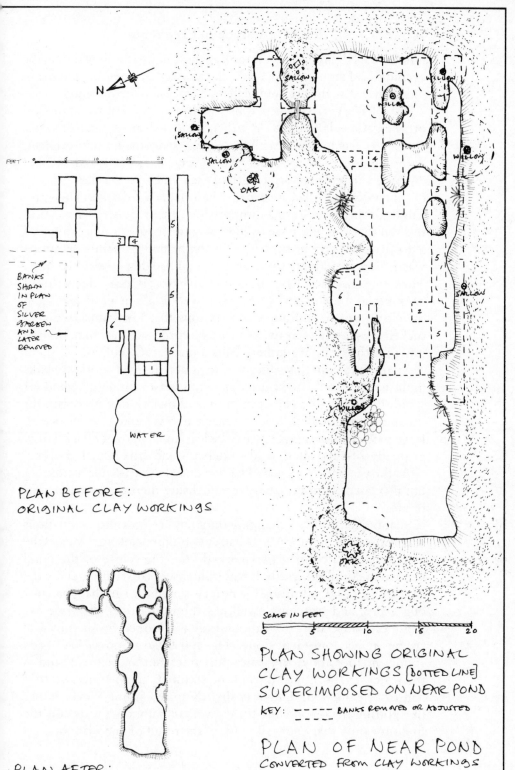

N

FEET ... 0   5   10   15   20

BANKS
SHOWN
IN PLAN
OF
SILVER
GARDEN
AND
LATER
REMOVED

WATER

PLAN BEFORE:
ORIGINAL CLAY WORKINGS

SALLOW

SALLOW

SALLOW

OAK

WILLOW

WILLOW

WILLOW

SALLOW

WILLOW

OAK

SCALE IN FEET
0   5   10   15   20

PLAN SHOWING ORIGINAL
CLAY WORKINGS [DOTTED LINE]
SUPERIMPOSED ON NEAR POND
KEY: ----- BANKS REMOVED OR ADJUSTED

PLAN OF NEAR POND
CONVERTED FROM CLAY WORKINGS

D.C.H.

PLAN AFTER:
NEAR POND

numbered "1" on the map. It took a whole day to remove, but in the evening, as I stood on the bank, the amount of pond I could see in one glance was almost double that I had seen in the morning.

It still had a narrow wasp-waist, so the next job was to cut the end off the peninsula marked "2"; then I had a clear expanse of water about fifty feet long and with an average width of about fifteen feet. After digging away the other two traverse banks (marked "3" and "4") the whole sixty yard length of the pond was laid clear.

I then decided that, as usual, I had made a mistake. The extra length of the pond gave an impression of extra narrowness, and I realised that I would have to dig away the long spit marked "5". I had started to earth up the strip of water behind it, mainly because it was a convenient place to throw the soil I had dug away elsewhere. Thus, not only did I have to remove an extra sixteen cubic yards of banking, and each cubic yard of soil weighs about a ton, but I had the chagrin of re-shifting about six tons that I had already dug. I tucked most of this soil away in various corners of the pond, or used it to give the straight southern bank a few natural bulges.

My last effort in this water was to attack the grid-work of banks in the eastern end. By this time my enthusiasm for digging and for stainless-steel spades had been mitigated by lack of enthusiasm for staggering about with loaded wheelbarrows, and so I decided to leave parts of these ridges as arty little islands, upon which I would grow lily-of-the-valley, wild strawberry and ornamental grasses.

As the years have gone by I have reduced these islands in number but increased them in size by cannibalising their unwanted neighbours.

Shaping the pond by changing the straight edges into undulations was also a pleasant job. After I had cut off the enclosing wings of the little square patch of water marked "6", the centre of the pond seemed to double in width. It was immensely satisfying to sit by the edge of the pond, admiring the neat curves of the rim that I had just dug away, and watching swallows skimming over the wide expanse of water. But, even though the job looked finished by late spring, it was only half done. The soil I had removed had been about one foot above the water plus an extra foot below it, and as the water level dropped during the summer, so an extra two foot had to be removed. This was slightly unrewarding work, rather like putting the second and third layers of paint on a wall, it is the first time only that one really can see the result of one's labours.

On page 66 there is a map of the settling pans. Most of the banks average four and a half feet in height, six to eight feet in width at the base and four to three feet at the top.

(I still use feet and inches, this being the system of Nature; my body does not conform to this wretched system of metric, invented by that murderous dwarf, Napoleon. My height and span are exactly six foot, my feet are one foot long – size 10 – and I have a useful finger joint which I can use to measure inches. I resent not being allowed to use the painfully learned measurements starting from 3 barleycorns equalling one inch right through to three miles equalling one league.)

To get back to the earthworks: they were rigidly artificial, they were also untidy and they broke up the smooth, continuous swarth out of which I intended the birches to grow. I therefore decided to remove them and unite all the pans into one level area, to diminish the steepness of any boundary banks that remained, so that they could be cut by mower rather than sickle, and to run the whole expanse of the "Silver Garden", as I now called it, right up to the waters of the Near Pond. This would therefore involve the removal of the bank separating the pond from the pans as well as the dividing banks within the pans. I calculated that this earth-shifting involved about one hundred and fifty tons, but as I intended to live there for the rest of my life I felt that there was no hurry, and I could do it at leisure. However, once started on something, one can become besotted by it: weekend after weekend I dug, sometimes even reluctant to answer Dominie's shouts of "lunch is ready" or the children's "Dr Who is just starting."

It was much harder work than it had been in the pond, for large tree stumps hung on to the banks with thick, writhing roots. I snapped the handle of one spade and the shafts of two axes – clumsy workmanship on my part, combined with irritated frenzy – and another spade, with a plastic handle, gave me electric shocks because of the friction. I now try only to buy tools which have got wooden handles: apart from generating electricity, plastic handles become slippery with sweat – though wooden ones can sometimes be insufficiently slippery which is why one spits on one's hands before using an axe. Nevertheless, the work was very satisfying as the view slowly opened up. The soil dug away was used to shape other areas, or to fill in ditches and hollows; the steep, cliff-like banks around the area were changed into long, gentle slopes, and a

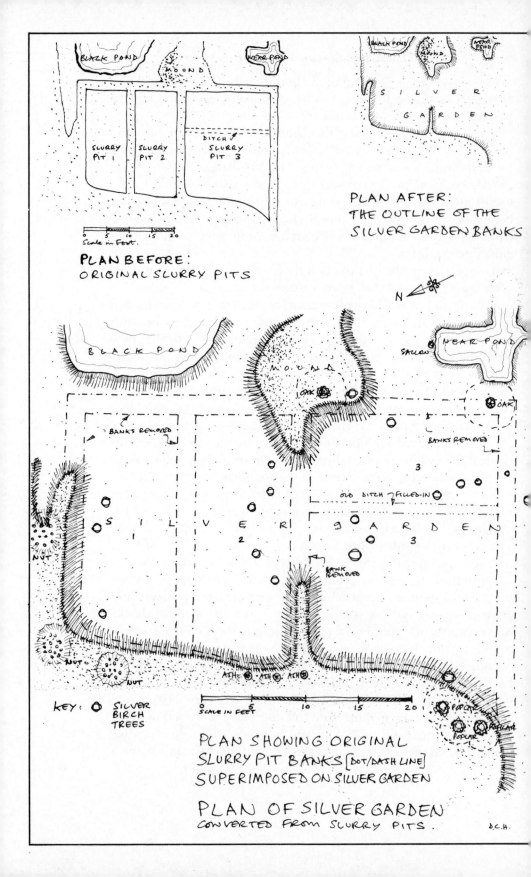

BLACK POND

MOUND

NEAR POND

SLURRY PIT 1

SLURRY PIT 2

DITCH
SLURRY PIT 3

0 5 10 15 20
Scale in Feet

PLAN BEFORE:
ORIGINAL SLURRY PITS

BLACK POND

MOUND

NEAR POND

S I L V E R

G A R D E N

PLAN AFTER:
THE OUTLINE OF THE
SILVER GARDEN BANKS

N

BLACK POND

MOUND

OAK

SALLOW

NEAR POND

OAK

BANKS REMOVED

BANKS REMOVED

3

OLD DITCH FILLED-IN

NUT

S I L V E R I G A R D E N

2 3

BANK REMOVED

NUT

NUT

ASH ASH ASH

POPLAR

POPLAR

POPLAR

KEY: ○ SILVER BIRCH TREES

0 5 10 15 20
SCALE IN FEET

PLAN SHOWING ORIGINAL
SLURRY PIT BANKS [DOT/DASH LINE]
SUPERIMPOSED ON SILVER GARDEN

PLAN OF SILVER GARDEN
CONVERTED FROM SLURRY PITS.

D.C.H.

hard, right-angled corner was padded out to make a sweeping curve.

One day Dominie decided to have a swimming pool. I disagreed, reckoning that we could not afford one and even if we could it would be a waste of money, as the only pleasure in swimming is in a river or when one puts on goggles and inspects the fish. I disagreed even more when she said she wanted it outside the kitchen, so that she could keep an eye on the children swimming while she was busy inside; I pointed out that I had just started up a small vegetable garden there, that I utterly refused to have a hole dug where Bell and I had spent a lot of hard work perfecting the soil, and that Rosie the donkey would have nowhere to graze.

Rosie lived in an enclosure which I had built for her behind the house. She spent almost all her time gazing meaningfully through the open kitchen window, and grew fat on toast. Mr Ryan told me that donkeys are the only animals which are stupid enough instinctively to like the human race and Rosie was certainly extremely affectionate. Once, when I was sitting on a bale talking to her, her eyes took on a dreamy expression and she clambered upon my lap, like an impulsive secretary, treading on all manner of sensitive areas before she was sitting comfortably. Whenever I moved her to better but more distant grazing, her plaintive but powerful brays could be heard all over the valley. If she was tethered in the Back Lawn she would walk round and round at the end of her rope until she had worn circular ruts in my precious new grass: many an archaeologist has excitedly dashed off to the site of a new ring-barrow which he has seen in the latest air-survey photographs, only to find that the crop-mark was caused by a rotating donkey or goat.

A swimming pool was built.

An enormous yellow machine first arrived, worked by a diminutive and extremely skilful driver. The machine had a fanged scoop on a long arm at one end and a shovel-cum-bucket on the other.

One day, as I was digging the last ten yards of bank, the tiny driver walked over and stood critically examining my efforts. I grew irritable, knowing what he was thinking.

At last he spoke. "Take you a week to do that lot, won't it?"

"About," I agreed sourly.

"Take me less with my digger. I'll do it if you like."

I was torn between relief and reluctance. I had just struck a very large and thick root, it would be ridiculous not to accept his offer, but I felt a sort of possessive this-is-all-my-own-workness. Common-sense overcame vanity and the big machine lurched towards the bank, snuggled itself down on its hydraulic legs, and in one bite took out enough soil to have kept me busy for twenty minutes.

Within an hour the bank had been removed, the earth had been landscaped against another bank, the driver was £2 richer and I was left to brood on the futility of my previous efforts.

But on looking back on it all, I am glad that most of it had been dug by myself. When I wander through the Silver Garden I know that it owes most of its appearance to the efforts of my own muscles. This is similar to the attitude I have about the trees I have planted. I have planned woods, decided on their sites, shapes and composition, and then named them. But I have not planted them personally, and therefore get more satisfaction out of the small isolated clumps which I have created with my own hands.

Whilst all this digging was in progress, some of our weekend guests were busy at the Far Pond.

It is my theory, probably as a result of laziness, that weekend guests should amuse themselves except during mealtimes and in the evenings. If they want their intellects kept busy they can borrow a book, visit Colchester museum, go to Cambridge or inspect the local churches; if they are talkative they can join Dominie in the kitchen; if they are idle they can lie in bed and if they are perfect they can ask what help is needed in the garden. I quickly discovered that if my answer was: "you can help dig away this bank", the reaction was extremely long faces followed by apologies for incapacitating tennis-elbows, ruptures or weak hearts. On the other hand, if I handed them an axe or a rip, they sprang into the wood like young beavers and hacked away all weekend.

Only a small part of the verges of the Far Pond was originally clear of scrub. This was just big enough for a fisherman to wiggle his rod. Personally, I think that if one is obliged to eat fish, and the only reason for eating most coarse fish must be starvation or ulcers, then the maximum equipment needed to catch them is a hand-grenade and a net. Others seem to think differently, and I give some of these eccentrics permission to catch the crucian carp which live in the Far Pond. Sometimes I go and stare at them in fascination: quite often they are children; small boys who normally spend their time yelling and breaking things suddenly change into mute statues, their heads enveloped in swarms of midges and their eyes rapt on the murky waters.

Within a year my guests had opened up two large glades on the sides of the pond. These guests approached this work with a variety of attitudes. Robert, being a Shetland Islander, detests trees. He had never seen one in his childhood, and the first few that came to his notice had not impressed him: he thought them tall and untidy. The army taught him more about the subject and he now knows that there are two sorts: "bushy-topped" and "pointed". He set about them with his axe in a way which would have made his Viking ancestors smile with appreciation.

Charles, a London friend, is different. There are various heroes on the television who remain miraculously neat under the most difficult conditions: people cosh them from behind in dark alley-ways, they fall groaning into heaps of dustbins, they stagger to their feet and fight off the murderous assaults of a dozen short, dark little villains and they finally escape by rolling over the bonnet of the chief baddy's on-coming car; a scene later they are strolling non-chalantly through the windows of their girlfriend's flat with their hair as neat and glossy as if it had been enamelled, their ties dangling decorously between uncreased lapels, and not a bag in sight about their trouser knees. Charles is like that. He goes into a thicket, crashes and batters inside it for an hour or so, and re-emerges looking as if he had just changed to take a rich aunt out to tea at the Ritz.

Gregory, on the other hand, emerges from the wood like an angry ape. He is an actor, and when dressed as some imaginary Detective Inspector or Tudor Baron he looks reasonably human; when bared for action in the woods he discloses a heavy matting of black hair on his chest and back: I sometimes wonder if he is going to hold the axe with his hands or with his feet.

Hamish, one of my six brothers-in-law, is a true Yorkshireman and the question of money runs persistently through his mind. He keeps interrupting his work to glower at me and say: "You realise that you'd have to be paying someone £1.50 an hour to do this?" After a while, the injustice of it all becomes too much, he flings down his axe and goes muttering towards the house and a drink.

Wilhelm is a large, red-faced Dutchman. His nervous suspicion of wild life looks incongruous when compared to his Teutonic beefiness. He has a sneaky feeling that blackthorns are like porcupines, and can shoot their prickles into his frame from a distance, that bumblebees, like bullets, have names written on them, and most of those names are his, and that the grass snakes, which are numerous, will fascinate him with their beady stare into walking down their gaping maws. He rarely sallies out alone further than fifty yards from the house.

When it was at last possible to stand in a large clearing by the Far Pond, it became even more obvious how overgrown it was, and how cluttered by fallen timber. Half-submerged willows and aspens reached despairing arms up to their overhanging cousins still standing on the banks. A small island in the middle was a tangle of brushwood and nettles, it completely blocked the view across the pond from every aspect. The water was of a dark greenish-brown, and so stagnant that on hot days fish lay lolling on the surface gulping for oxygen. A large patch of water-lilies was the only attractive object.

The bed of the pond was covered by a thick layer of ooze, a mixture of dead leaves, rotten branches, clay and humus which had crumbled from the banks. My two pet horrors are spiders and quicksands and the engulfing sucking-in action of this ooze reminded me unpleasantly of a quicksand I had once stepped in by Findhorn Bay. I lost my rubber boots several times in this mud, but only once did I feel in real danger. I was then wearing thigh boots, which made me less nimble in my efforts to escape, and as I waded desperately away from the mud I sank further and further in until the sludge was over-topping my boots. Fortunately, by then, I had managed to reach the overhanging branch I was aiming for, and I heaved myself out of my boots. As I lay panting along the branch I heard my abandoned footwear filling up with water below me with a sound that incongruously reminded me of Pimms No 1 being poured from a jug into a tankard.

It is probable that my panic was unjustified and that the mud was not as deep as I thought. I remember watching a man punting up the Cam when I was an undergraduate. He had his wife and children in the punt with him and was understandably showing-off the techniques of his youth: his sleeves rolled up, his bare feet splayed at the correct stance, his punt pole sliding freely through his hand after each shove. He had even remembered how to do all this without water running down his arms: he had forgotten, however, that parts of the riverbed are overlaid with sticky mud, and his pole

stuck in a patch of it. He made the old mistake of hanging on instead of letting go. At the last moment, when he was overbalanced and the onlookers were delightedly waiting for him to hit the water he abandoned the pole, the punt and his progeny by leaping upwards and by a remarkable bit of dexterity he managed to grab the branch of a weeping willow. There he hung, lugubriously, like a discarded piece of washing. Slowly the branch bent under his weight, and the water touched his toes. He drew his legs up. Still the branch continued to sag. He drew his knees up to his chin – we watched in breathless silence, there was no malice in us and we wished him well, but we wished him wet – no avail to his efforts, the clammy waters of the Cam crept up his crouched body until they reached his chin. With resignation he released the bough and prepared to swim. It was not necessary, the river was only two feet deep. Applause and cheers broke out from the on-lookers as he stood up, several people called out "Thank you, Thank you" in voices full of genuine gratitude and an agitated undergraduate next to me on the bridge called out sadly, "Please could you do it again, I didn't see it all?"

Once the glades had been cleared on the banks of the Far Pond there was room to stack the trash from the water. First to go was the growth from the "island". I call it an island, but in fact it is only one during the driest two months, when a few square yards break the surface, for the rest of the year it is submerged. I used to paddle out to it in a rubber dinghy, and paddle back towing bundles of brushwood behind me. Once it was cleared the full expanse of the water could be seen, but like all clearing it revealed further nastiness. This time it was the enormous amount of dead branches which stuck out of the water. Some of these could be removed as they still joined on to the trunks of fallen trees whose butts remained on the banks, but even this proved difficult in many cases, particularly with the willows which had decided that though fallen they were not beaten and had grown thick bundles of matted roots, like fibrous beards, which gripped the pond bed. In the winter, the pond iced over, and my task was simplified: I could wander over the surface of the pond and saw off the branches which showed above the ice. This did not make the pond any better for the fishermen, but it made it look much neater. I kept a couple of dead branches in position as they were interestingly contorted and were also well-placed perches for reed buntings, warblers and other small birds.

The Near Pond

Candy thinks that one of these branches is the claw of a dragon and sidles past it, nervously alert for any sign of movement.

All overhanging branches were cleared to about eight feet above the ice. The moorhens did not like their skulks being removed but, when the sun appeared and the ice thawed, the dappled effect of the leaves in the shaded water was very pleasant. Partly because of the removal of so much rotten wood, but mainly because of the effect of extra light, the water became much less cloudy and stagnant and one could see, in the spring, small shoals of fish drifting beneath the surface. When they jumped, ripples expanded their rings from bank to bank and rebounded in a collection of moving, interlocking arcs. The children could play ducks-and-drakes or could scramble along the banks looking for the empty shells of fresh-water mussels.

I became rather excited about these mussels, because I read in a local paper about a man who owned a stretch of water full of pearl mussels. The fresh-water pearl can be superior to the sea pearl; the best are a glowing pinkish-yellow, though they can be white, brown or even green, and large ones are very rare and expensive. George and I therefore dredged up a few of our own mussels and opened them up. This was a disgusting occupation, as their shells averaged six to seven inches in length and every inch was packed with slimy flesh. No pearls were found, and Monk told me later that our molluscs are the large swan mussels, the smaller pearl mussels prefer to live in more oxygenated water. Neither of them are worth eating. The only garden molluscs I have tried as food are the large garden snails.

"Well I'm blessed!" cried Hart in amazement on entering the kitchen and spying the remains of our *Escargots à la Bourguignonne* on the table, "you've been a-dining on hod-me-dods!"

I could sympathise with his queasy startlement. I felt the same when we rented a holiday bungalow in Corsica: small snails used to creep to the tops of the heather during any rainfall and our gardener used to rush out with a bag and harvest them, whilst his wife seethed sauces in preparation, anticipation and the kitchen.

Most of our snails are the ordinary garden snail, and various parts of the Formal Garden have heaps of their empty shells beside the anvils which thrushes use to batter them against. I have also found the striped shells of banded snails, mainly in yellows and browns, but sometimes with black, beiges and gingers. For some reason, I have often found collections of snail shells among the dry, cavernous hollows at the foot of old trees, perhaps these are the dining rooms of shrews, who eat them in large quantities.

There are about eighty species of land snail in Britain, including bubble-like glass snails, cylindrical door snails and even hairy snails: I shall make a closer study of the varieties in the garden; meanwhile it is the slugs which take up most of my attention. When he was four, Charlie kept a vast black one in a bucket and fed it on lettuce. He called it Saint Jim.

The Mangrove Swamp was originally a hodge-podge of pits and sunken depressions. About half an acre had been dug in this way by the clay workers, to an average depth of five feet. At the far south, alongside the Pinetum, the diggings had dwindled to a halt in such a way as to show their method of working, which was to excavate rows of pans about ten foot square, and then to unite them. This whole complex was entirely taken over by willows: dead, dying or thriving; some only a year old, others with five foot girths. The water averaged only a foot and a half in depth, but was almost completely obscured by the tangled mass of trash.

Having seen the difference I had made in the Far Pond, I decided to attack this area in a similar manner, but as work progressed my policy changed. For one thing, it became obvious that no strong sunlight would reach the water unless I completely felled the Pinetum: its dark shadow overhung much of the space; in addition, the tall hedge to the east would have to be razed; I had no wish to remove either; above all, once the dead and fallen timber had been cleared, the living willows made intriguing and pleasant clumps as they grew out of the water. Each clump consisted of about a dozen stems: I cleared them of their lower twigs, and their undulating boles now wriggled down to their reflections in the amber-coloured shallows.

After the rip, saw, axe and bonfire, the spade was brought into action once more. I firstly dug away the remaining ridges which encompassed the pans in the southern part, thus opening up another two hundred and forty square yards into the main sheet of water. Next I levelled off the steep adjacent bank so that there was a gradual, sloping expanse of land leading down from the Pinetum to the water's edge. This was done simply, by digging away the soil at the top of the bank and throwing it down to the bottom, letting winter's frosts break up the clods, and then raking it smooth. There were three very big hawthorns growing on this bank and I left them untouched having first cleared the soil around their roots to the level of the newly exposed land beside them. They now stand on clusters of exposed roots in an intriguing – if not particularly pretty – manner.

As I worked northwards in the Mangrove Swamp I found, at the top, that a long spit of water extended to the west. One day I scrambled and slithered among the branches that blocked this channel and eventually discovered, to my surprise, that I had emerged into a still, thorn-ringed pool about fifty feet in diameter. I waded across it and with some difficulty pushed through the thorn for about ten feet until I broke through and found myself in the Silver Garden. I think that this is good evidence to show how thick some of the undergrowth in the wood has been: it had taken two years before I found a pond only one hundred yards from my back door.

The thorn was cleared from the perimeter, which laid bare yet another bank. This I dug away and now, when standing on part of the Back Lawn, it is possible to see this pool, the Black Pond, its dark waters a sombre background for the silver trunks of the birches.

The land between the Black Pond and the Mangrove Swamp was considerably higher than the rest of the garden. I decided to clear it of the thorn and scrub, but to leave the larger and better-spaced trees, mostly oak but also a few ashes and willows, so that their high canopy would spread noticeably and impressively above the rest of the garden. As I worked I discovered the reason for the height of the area, it marked the site of the old pug mill where the clay had been puddled in a round pit before it was run off into the pans below. I could still see the circular track about the perimeter which had been worn down by the bored hooves of the ponies who had had to turn the heavy wooden beam which stirred the sludge. Unlike the rest of the garden, the soil here is light and sandy, and a rabbit warren covers part of its sloping shoulders. Below, to the north, it levels out, and there I have done only a little clearing, and have planted bluebells amongst the dogwood and willows.

My last effort with landscaping was to extend the raised causeway which separated the Near Pond from the Mangrove Swamp. This ran for thirty yards and then fell into a deep hollow. I filled this in with earth from part of the warren and thus extended the causeway to a total length of forty-five yards. I have planted an avenue of weeping willows along it; in ten years' time it should be a golden tunnel.

Mangrove Swamp

CHAPTER 5

The flowers and shrubs

Whilst I was busy in the recesses of the wood, Dominie was fossicking about with the flower beds.

During the war, some friends of my father's had to look after the queen of a country which had been invaded by the Germans. On the day that she arrived at their house the rooms had been filled with flowers to make her feel at home and welcome. She graciously entered the front door, smiling affably at the servants lined up to meet her and then stiffened, sniffing. Casting a cold look at the massed array of bloomage before her, she said:

"Flowers in zer garten, ver goot; flowers in zer house, zey stink."

While not being as indifferent to flowers as this queen, I have a strong preference for trees and shrubs: I prefer large objects and am unable to "swoop earthwards", as Beverley Nichols exhorts us, in order to gaze upwards into the smiling face of some violet or pansy; also trees and shrubs, once established, need little attention, unlike flowers which need their beds weeded, their clumps divided and their seed-pods dead-headed.

Thus when dealing with flowers I tend to concentrate on the establishment of naturalised bulbs, which as a task is an off-shoot of my landscaping and tree planting, and Dominie concentrates on the flower beds.

The Rose Garden is divided up into groups of four by two wide walks which cross it at right-angles, and each group, in its turn, is quartered by smaller walks making a total of sixteen plots. Some colour co-ordination had originally been planned: pinks and reds, yellows and salmons, whites and yellows, reds and oranges. Of all

78

these, only the Queen Elizabeth looked healthy. There were many blank spaces where dead bushes had been removed, and after we had added to this desolation by removing even more dead or ailing shrubs Dominie estimated that at least six dozen more would have to be planted. While she deliberated, the remaining roses took a remarkable turn for the better thanks to a combination of extra soil, manure, weeding and pruning, the latter being particularly concerned with the removal of suckering briars from the parent root-stocks and paring down some of the bushes which had grown to over five feet. Being then ignorant of such things, I was appalled to see the initial effect of the pruning of Dominie and Bell: where once a mass of branches had tangled, a collection of short, spiny fingers jabbed out of the layers of horse and cow manure; about three weeks later, however, all these stumps had sprouted new red shoots which raced towards the sun and burst into flower during May and June.

Pruning has always been a vexed question: Bell preferred it done in the late autumn, so that the plants would not lose sap which might happen during a spring pruning, but Hart reckons that they should be untouched until the winter is over so that the leaves can feed the roots as long as possible and because the frosts will kill only the superfluous tips of the stems rather than the important new growth further down. From the experience in our garden, Hart's theory is the better, but conditions could be different elsewhere.

I was surprised to learn that roses are closely related to a wide variety of plants, ranging from brambles to medlars. The family groupings in the living world are particularly interesting, potatoes are in the same family as tomatoes and deadly nightshade, skates are flattened sharks, octopi are shell-less snails, badgers are related to bears and weasels, the sparrow is not a sort of finch as I supposed but Britain's only weaver bird, the dodo was a sort of pigeon and some whales are streamlined hippopotamuses; perhaps oddest of all is that the bat, being related to the lemur, is probably the British animal most closely related to man.

Dominie decided to concentrate on floribundas in the Rose Garden because of their ability to produce an effect of massed colour. Hybrid tea roses were planted amongst these, mainly for their scent and their virtue as excellent flowers for cutting. Whilst at her orgy of rose ordering, Dominie also bought roses for the herbaceous borders, the crescent bed, the Back Lawn and the walls of the house.

The herbaceous borders were planted with species roses for their impression of wild magnificence, their large size, and their "easy-care" properties. Most of them have thrived superbly, and the only attention necessary is the removal of suckers from a few and the staking up of a couple of them which became top-heavy: perhaps we had put too much sand in the places where they grow. We planted many too far forward as we did not know that they would become so big – Frühlingsgold, for example, had grown about seven feet high and wide in three years, and now most of the others have reached that size. The general effect of the herbaceous border is therefore more of a rose walk, and many of the smaller flowers can only be seen between the bushes when one stands next to them; as we think that the roses are much prettier, we do not mind.

When planning for the Back Lawn, Dominie was mentally looking over the village to the Park, a house whose garden contains magnificent clumps of rhododendrons. The local soil is not suitable for these so one of the Edwardian inhabitants of that house dug huge pits about fifty feet across, and three feet deep, and filled them with acid soil. These are now large groups of shrubbery, well-placed on the three-acre lawn. The two other places I have been to which have superb rhododendrons are the estate of Altyre, in Morayshire, where the shrubs planted by Sir William Gordon-Cumming have spread in mile-long arcades and climb in multi-coloured sweeps of colour from a little burn to banks forty foot high, and Portmeirion, where a sort of mini-Portofino has been built amongst the relics of a much older garden. Some of the rhododendrons there are as high as oaks and one has flower clusters as big as footballs, with large leaves backed by a furry brown covering which looks like the best suede. Portmerion was designed by Clough Williams-Ellis in an extraordinary mixture of Italian styles which somehow merge together well on the Welsh hillside. I had two particular pleasures when I stayed there: grovelling, possibly illegally, in an old gold mine – and finding a bit of quartz with the glitter of gold in it, and lying in bed in the Watch-tower, the hotel cottage we had taken, and looking through the window beside me over two miles of the bay of Traeth Bach. When the tide was out I could see shellduck and waders prodding and shovelling among the exposed sandbanks; when the tide was in, merganzers and other divers swam and dipped in the waters eighty feet below me. I met Williams–Ellis, a handsome and entertaining old man in his nineties; he told me that he first learned his architectural trade, as a boy, from a man who had been born in 1798.

Back to the roses. Having admired our neighbours' clusters of rhododendrons, but having no intention of digging pits fifty foot across, we decided that the shrub rose type would be suitable for clumping on the Back Lawn.

Beside this group of shrubs Dominie planted a climber against the adjacent pear tree; more climbers were put against the walls of the house and out-buildings, not just roses, but other plants such as clematis, whose flowers make an attractive comparison to those of the roses and, most striking of all, the Passion Flower, which grows around the front door. It is meant to be delicate, but it has grown rapidly with no die-back and often does so here until mid-December; its flowers fascinate all those who see it, with their ten greenish white petals representing the "Nimbus", or halo of Christ, the black, white and blue filaments of the corona representing the Crown of Thorns, the five anthers the five wounds suffered on the Cross and the three styles the three nails.

Dominie's arrangement of roses for the Crescent Border is especially effective: three different heights, seven feet, four feet and eighteen inches merge together to form one magnificent cascade, the white crests of Iceberg standards tumbling down to a flurry of pinks and salmons which then fall into a foam-like froth of cherry-red dwarf Ellen Poulsens. Purple and red aubretia then carry the edge of the tide in wavelets which lap on to the shingle path.

I am slightly less enthusiastic about the weeping roses that Dominie has placed as sentinels at the entrance of the herbaceous border; they sound pleasant in theory, but in fact they need a large amount of ironmongery to make them behave: pipes three inches in diameter and five feet high poke out of the ground and are sur-mounted by hats which look like skeletonic umbrellas. The roses are meant to hide these, but totally fail to do so in winter, and even when in leaf there are generally enough bare patches left to show the metal beneath. They catch the wind and become lop-sided; during a tempest one rose broke into a frenzy of hipswinging, like a hula-hula dancer, and finally gyrated itself off its stem.

The Formal Garden

I have never been very keen on garden ornaments in country gardens. I can tolerate a summerhouse if it has been designed by Wren or Repton, or a bridge – if it is really being used as a bridge and not just plonked at the end of a lake. It seems pointless to have urns or pots scattered about unless one has a town house where there is a shortage of earth, or if one wants to grow something which will not tolerate one's own soil. Even this seems to be a bit silly, because every soil has its own prima-donnas, and if one cannot grow rhododendrons or camellias, for example, why not concentrate on roses and peonies instead? Statues in a garden leave me even colder: they are generally expensive substitutes for plastic gnomes. One of my great-aunts had a particularly large statue which may have kinked my infant mind into this adult dislike. I vividly remember the first time that I saw it. Her garden had a meandering of dark, gloomy paths flanked by tall yew hedging. I happened to be creeping furtively down one after tea one day. Tea was always a painful ritual, dominated by the pouring of a huge silver teapot, a vast ornate contraption squatting, with the help of a complicated stand, over a small heater which barely kept its behind warm. From its bulbous and baroque sides a very long and thin spout protruded which, when used, emitted a minute stream of pale yellow fluid which poured for an agonisingly long time into each cup, with a tinny and reedy tinkle; this invariably made any children present burst into nervous titters.

As I rounded the corner of one of the paths I came face to face with a colossal marble woman, naked as a worm except for a tuft of moss and a pair of sandals. She held someone's severed head in one hand, the other hand hovered genteely over the moss. Although full of shocked surprise that my great-aunt should have such a rude person in her garden, I was nevertheless highly intrigued by this disclosure of the female form, and from then on would frequently visit my aged relation in order to see her stoney companion. In the end I became quite anxious about the statue, standing so cold and forlorn among the yews.

Our own statues are three squat lead urchins who live in the Rose Garden. They represent Water, Spring and Autumn, and must have been part of a larger group. They have fat leaden cheeks and eyes that peer blankly from puffy features; their bodies are enveloped in rolls of fat and scarves, these garments are hung over one shoulder in the manner of a Scotchman's plaid, and are artfully arranged so as to frame their blubbery bosoms and "privates", as Bell called them. My dislike of them increased when Joanna, a neighbour, placed herself in front of Water, the one with the largest face and smallest "private", examined it critically, examined me, and then turned to Dominie saying: "Well, I see why you got that one."

Our other ornaments are an assortment of urns. We bought five of these as a result of an advertisement in a local paper. When Dominie and I turned up at the given address we were disconcerted to see a large policeman in the garden; however, as he was one of the friendly ones in a pointed hat – rather than a disagreeable one in a flat hat and a motor car – we proceeded down the garden path and asked him who was selling the urns. "I am," he said, which surprised me, as I did not know that the police went in for what the army calls "extra-anus" activities. His urns turned out to be crucibles for melting metal. They are made of plumbago, which is not only a small evergreen shrub, but also an amalgam of lead, graphite and clay. They are smooth, greyish and rather unnoticeable, and thus do not distract attention from the plants which grow in them. In the smaller ones, which are about one and a half feet high, Dominie plants annuals such as wallflowers; in the ones which are three feet high she has planted camellias and azaleas, shrubs which hate our soil. These plants looked very miserable for a year until we were told that as the plants do not like our alkaline soil, they will not like our alkaline water either, now that Dominie collects water from a rain butt, they thrive.

Bell died.

He did so suddenly one night. There was no reason for it and we almost felt cross with him for leaving us without warning. He was only seventy-seven but, as his mother said sadly at his funeral: "I always thought he'd never make old bones."

The garden seemed like an abandoned room; I kept looking up from my work to ask his advice and then remembering that he was gone; Dominie, cutting flowers, half expected to see him in the rusty black suit he always wore, delving about with a hoe nearby.

We still miss him.

James Hart, the former orchard keeper and one of Bell's first friends, volunteered to take his place. He is like his old friend in many ways: he also had become bored by retirement, he too is full of country lore and knowledge and although not prone to moments of melancholy he has Bell's other ability suddenly to burst into fits of merriment, usually about "folks and their rum ways".

One of his first tasks was to deal with an urn that Dominie had bought. It was a large stone object which filled Hart and me with foreboding when we first saw it, and we forebade correctly: it wandered all over the garden looking for a suitable place to live, and it was we who had to move its nine heavy segments from place to place. It started off by standing on the edge of the Near Pond. After a day or so, Dominie decided that it looked too precarious there, so Hart and I were told to lug it to the centre of the Silver Garden; it stood there incongruously, like a neat stockbroker in a jungle. After summer it travelled back to the centre of the Back Lawn, hesitated for a week, had a look into the end of the swimming pool and finally made up its mind and settled in the middle of the Rose Garden, where it blocks the view down the ride. But it is a pretty shape, and the aubretia and thyme that Dominie plants in it look attractive cascading down its mossy sides. Its greatest improvement happened when George, playing hide-and-seek, knocked it over and shattered its centre segment, this diminished it by a foot in height without, in my opinion, spoiling its symmetry.

For some time two half-tubs stood by the front door. I thought that they made the house look "towny", but the more I painted them, the more out of place they looked. I had seen some looking very attractive in a London mews, painted white with the metal hoops in black, but this did not suit our surroundings; when painted black all over, they stood out and distracted attention from the flowers they contained; when painted green, they looked as if they were camouflaging themselves in embarrassment. Their hoops kept slipping down like badly-fitting bras, and it was with pleasure that I saw a friend backing his car into one after dinner, splitting it open like a melon. They ended up as kindling wood, and Dominie replaced them with a pair of terra-cotta tubs whose colour merges reasonably with the brickwork of the house.

The beds in front of the house were also planted with roses, but these were augmented with the pot bulbs bought or given at Christmas. The bulbs, having completed their objective in the house, are expelled into the open air and although never as fine again still look very pleasant, mainly because of vigorous dead-heading. Most of them are hyacinths, and appear in early spring before the roses can hide them with their leaves; their scent, particularly in the evening, is very powerful and most welcome when I return from the smells of London after work.

Crown imperials also grow in these beds. Candy is fascinated by the circle of crystal beads hidden in each drooping head; tears of regret that they were too proud to bow, as did all the other flowers, when Jesus passed on his way to the Cross. On a more mundane note, some people dislike them for their smell of fox.

We had a fox once, a vixen we called Fenella. She arrived as a cub and resembled a long-legged rat. Her brush was snakey and thin, her muzzle quivered with apprehensive curiosity, her pelt was short and sleek. She became very tame, and would run along the tops of the sofas and nibble our ears and mew affectionately. However, if she was handled too roughly by the children, or if one stood on her brush by mistake – and this often happened as she would lie under a chair with it sticking out – she would whirl round and embed her needle-like fangs into us. As she grew older, so she grew more reluctant to stay indoors and eventually she lived the whole time in a nest she made in the hedge of the Rose Garden, and only came indoors for her meals. By the time she was six months old she was lithe and magnificent, her brush had fuzzed out and she played with her only friend amongst the dogs – which, rather quirkily, was Algy, the fox terrier – like a plume of chestnut coloured smoke as she wove around him and leapt over him. One day I found her dead in the Paddock: I think she had been poisoned. I grieved about this to Monk.

"Never mind," he said with gloomy resignation, "however many foxes die, there will always be one to turn up at the funeral."

Dominie decided to surround the swimming pool with blue to match the mosaic tiles in the water. A blue Lawson cypress was planted in one corner, next to the Pepper Pot, whose conical shape it compliments. Only a few blue-leaved plants grow along the north facing wall as blue leaves, like silver ones, seem to need good sunlight to compensate for their paucity of chlorophyll, but a Clematis Macropetala acts as substitute with a mass of violet-blue flowers. The other border faces east and Dominie planted spyrea and buddleia against it, fronting them with a line of cat-mint whose rounded mounds are used as cushions by Pandora and Millicent. A ceanothus lived up to its reputation of tenderness by dying soon after planting, but a variety of iris reticulata, whose flowers range in colour from pale blue to deep purple, with a golden strip in the middle, seem to flower well in shade or sun. Butterflies regard blues, mauves and then pinks as the most attractive of all colours, and it is this part of the garden that they are seen in the greatest numbers.

We have bought very few flowers for the garden, most of them have come as gifts from friends. This scrounging of mine is very productive during election time. I have been a District Councillor for about fifteen years, representing three parishes which cover an area of about eleven square miles. I am an Independent as I do not think that national politics are either necessary or useful at that low level, and I also consider that I should represent all the parishioners from the most rabid red to the most apoplectic blue. During the three weeks before each election day I traipse the lanes and village streets with my messages. I always notice, with despondence, that my rival candidates harangue the electorate knowledgeably on such subjects as bus timetables, the emptying of cesspits, the lack of visiting chiropodists and the need for more signposts; I, on the other hand, can only talk with authority on the weather, ground elder, the abilities – or otherwise – of the local doctors and vets in diagnosing ailments and the scandalous behaviour of local teenagers with either their motorbikes, if they are male, or their charms, if female.

Each of my calls usually necessitates a walk up a garden path to a back door – the front door is only used for carrying brides in and coffins out – and I am thus able to inspect the plants: if any seem attractive I can then beg, borrow or swap.

After about five years of planned rose planting and random flower planting, the herbaceous borders, which cover an area of 320 square yards, still had many blank spaces; these grew nothing but weeds. The garden began to overwhelm me with work. It took six back-breaking hours to mow the lawn with a non-self-propelled, 36″ Hayter; trimming all the hedges took three more days; it took two days to trim the hedges of the Rose Garden. I could only work during weekends; first Bell and now Hart have only worked for two days per week and although rapid workers, through both skill and inclination, their seventy years burdened them when any heavy duties were necessary.

I overcame some of these problems by buying better tools, the most notable being the tractor-mower. It not only made the task of cutting grass more pleasant – even the children like to do it – it also halved the time; as an extra bonus it is useful in various jobs around the farm. However, weeding remained the greatest problem, so Mr Barcock came to visit.

He is a spry man in ancient tweeds; a former rubber-planter who came to Suffolk from the Far East after retirement and, having bought a house with a wilderness around it, set about creating an extraordinarily fine garden and nursery on the solid clay. His speciality is ground-covering plants, particularly needed nowadays as there is a rapidly diminishing number of people who can afford full-time gardeners, and thus flower beds and herbaceous borders are being cleared of their time-consuming annuals and bedded-out flowers and planted, instead, with ground-covering plants which lessen the need for weeding, and with bushes which need little attention except for the occasional pruning.

He told me that there were several items to consider when planning a border, such as:
The height of each plant, obviously a tall plant must not hide a

shorter one but should be planted near the back of a border – or in the middle if it can be approached from both sides;

The season of the plant's colour – whether it be flower, foliage or fruit – one should ensure that there are no large expanses of blank greens from too many adjacent plants who have finished, or not yet started, their visual activity;

Colour co-ordination, similarly there should not be large patches of one colour, nor should colours which "swear" be planted close together. It is wrong to think that all the colours of Nature are compatible and I can remember many examples which disprove this convention, such as the eye-wrenching stripes of some tulip fields, the ginger beard and puce face of a local publican, the displeasing mottles of some fungi or the welter of colour in certain public gardens which specialise in "hospital" beds, inhabited by anaemic hydrangeas lying beside apoplectic begonias and choleric celosias;

Anti-social plants – those which may be attractive but which cannot get on with certain neighbours, privet, for example, which is greedy on the soil, barberries, which can give black rust to adjacent wheat fields, rampant spreaders such as Policeman's Helmet or shade-makers such as yew.

We planted about thirty different flowers and shrubs as a result of Mr Barcock's visit, some of these effective weed smotherers are mentioned in appendix D2.

They include ornamental grasses, and having seen how pleasant these can be, I began to take a greater interest in the grasses which grew wild round about me. I had originally been introduced to grasses when staying with a cousin of mine who had married a Transylvanian girl. She was a descendant of Vlad the Impaler, who, as Dracula, has had his good name grossly slandered by Hammer Films over the last few decades. She had a large tattooed snake on her right thigh, and being extremely rich, of mid-European excitability, and untrained to the niceties of Western etiquette, she was liable to spread astonishment, confusion and chaos during her erratic progress through life. When living in Grosvenor Square, for example, she kept some bush babies in a bidet in a spare bathroom. A famous composer and his mistress came to stay: the mistress was a massively built contralto. On their arrival at my cousin's house the songstress was overcome by that quaint urge which afflicts foreigners, namely a desire to sit on the bidet. (The British, being more decorous, only use bidets for washing their feet, or for drip-drying shirts.) Having sat on it, she was instantly surprised to feel the furtive fondling of tiny hands and, on looking down between her thighs, met the roguish gaze of three pairs of twinkling brown eyes. Her beautifully toned screams could be heard as far as Oxford Circus.

Great was the dourness and gloom, when my cousins bought a castle on the Western shores of Scotland. I do not remember anything odd happening when I stayed there at the age of ten, but I do remember one of the guests. He was a youngish, gangling man, dressed in knickerbockers, and he used to sally out after each breakfast with an intriguing tin case belted on to his back. One day my curiosity overcame my awe of adults and I asked to go with him. He cheerfully agreed. We traipsed along the cliff tops until suddenly he fell to his knees with a cry of triumph, tweaked out a piece of grass, and carefully lowered it into a compartment of his tin.

He was besotted about grasses and sedges.

Enthusiasm can be contagious, if the enthusiast has the ability to communicate. I do not remember much of those far off days when I walked under the pale blue skies with the tall man in knickerbockers, but sometimes the scent of sun-warmed thyme and turf, or the feel of an Atlantic breeze on my face brings back a flash of memory. However, I still remember some of the things that he told me: my surprise when I heard that bamboos were just large grasses, the delight which I felt on seeing that the puce-coloured seed heads of flea sedge really did look like fleas and my pride when I was able to distinguish a grass from a sedge: the former has a round cross section to its stem (which is usually hollow) and nodes where the leaves sprout from the plant, sedges are triangular and solid in their stems and have no nodes.

As the years passed my enthusiasm waned. I forgot the names I had learned till they became mere faint echoes which would sometimes ring in my empty skull. By the time we moved to Wastewood only flea sedge and cocksfoot were remembered and I had learned, in addition, about the dreaded activities of twitch, but then having been motivated by the sight of Mr Barcock's ornamental grasses, I bought a reference book on grasses and sedges. The most noticeable of such growth in the garden grows on the edges of all the marshy areas and ponds; clumps of a tall, dark-leaved sedge whose curving seed stems, bearing long drooping brown tails, arch from four to six feet: my book identified it as the pendulous sedge. Shadow does not seem to worry it and as it likes to grow beside water, it is a good nesting place for the ducks, especially mallard which can lurk unseen amongst the shaggy manes of leaves. I read, with insular pride, that it is a particular speciality of our area.

I found other sedges: the fuzzy bluish clumps of the glaucus sedge; in the drier, more shaded places, wood sedge, with vivid, pale leaves below a swarm of seeds; the scarce sedge, scarce in seeds rather than in numbers; cyperus sedge, with hanging seed heads like bristly green maize and my old friend the flea sedge, growing in the damp and mossy area of lawn near the beech hedge.

As my newly bought book also described grasses, I began to re-learn their names. I first looked up the name of a grass which grows particularly well in the Pinetum, sending up two-foot high stalks which arch with the weight of the seed heads, each of these with long whiskers so that the whole plant looks like a miniature fountain, or the sky-marks of a bursting rocket; this is the barren brome. I was next intrigued by a grass which grows on the south bank of the Near Pond. This bank had been almost vertical, but not quite steep enough to hinder a thick growth of thorn and dogwood which blocked the view from the water and the water from the sun. After I had cleared the scrub and shallowed the angle of the bank, the whole thirty yard stretch became a mass of pale green – almost golden – leaves, wood false-brome. It could be that the seeds of this grass have a long germination period and I was looking at the children of decades-old seeds, but I suspect that it was through the efficiency of its seed distribution; when I walk through the uncut grass in the early autumn the seeds shoot off from their cases in a most ungrass-like fashion and when working on the bank with a sickle I have to guard my eyes from the flying missiles. The ordinary wood brome also grows in the garden, with fuzzy stems up to 6 feet in height, from which branchlets sprout, holding their seeds and flowers close to the stem in spring and summer, and then arching them out before shedding. This emphasises one of the special problems of grasses, they can look very different in their stages of infancy, puberty, marriage, pregnancy, middle age and death, and reference books are inclined to illustrate them without indicating which stage is being portrayed.

My particular favourite amongst the grasses which grow in my

garden is the wood melick and I am so keen on it that I have
transplanted several clumps from their original home in the south
part of the Pinetum. Its long leaves are of a pale and juicy green. The
oval seeds are sparse but relatively large, about the size of a big
pinhead, and of a rich, dark chestnut. Each seed is at the end of a
stalk, so long and thin that even the slightest wind makes it bob up
and down and thus the whole colony looks like a swarm of little
brown beetles dancing above the woodland floor.

   Although I have an abundance of swampy areas, not many rushes
grow, and I once thought that this was because they need sunlight as
only their stems can collect chlorophyll, but I have since heard that
great forests of bull-rush live permanently submerged beneath the
waters of some of the lakes in the Lake District, and suffer no ill
effect in the murky light. What I called bull-rush in my childhood
was reedmace, a tall reed (a reed is merely a grass which grows in
damp places) with a long brown spike of seeds which look like a
ramrod: if you run your thumbnail down it in autumn, the fluffy
seeds spring away from the heads in a golden cascade. The real
bull-rush is a long tubular plant which can grow over six feet high.
It is stoloniferous, and can quickly spread in thick clumps which,
early in the season, look like a forest of dark green knitting needles

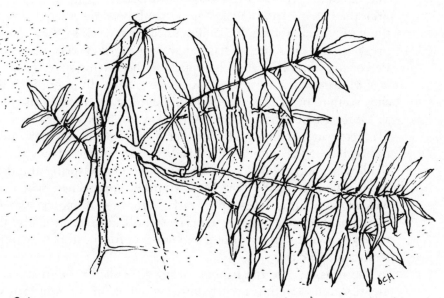

Rhus.

stabbing out of the water. Later, when taller, they bend, and in this position they seem to be particularly attractive to warblers as perches, perhaps they like the see-saw motion. The other rushes I have are a few soft rushes scattered about in the shallower parts of the Near Pond, jointed rush in the Mangrove Swamp and hard rush in a corner of the Pasture.

Having gone, so to speak, down to grass roots level, the subject of moss naturally occurs. Parts of my lawn are smothered in it and I treat it as I do the daisies and dandelions, with amiable indifference. I think it looks quite pleasant, and it is springy to walk on and comfortable to lie on; I also recognise its disadvantages; during dry seasons it withers and leaves large arid patches and in damper months the lawn-mower skims chunks of it off the surface. I therefore scratch at it with a wire rake when the feeling takes me, but this feeling does not take me very often. Most of the moss killers seem to contain worm killers as well, and I do not want to kill worms as they feed birds and aeriate the soil which, during the summer, can bake as hard as a parade ground. (A friend of mine, a wild and woolly Welshman, sneaks out at night with a torch and catches worms which lie dozing on the surface of his lawn. He then sews along their bodies with knitting wool until he has a length of worm several feet long. He throws the worms into his river, ties one end of the wool to a tree and goes to bed. During the night eels grab the worms and their insloping teeth become entangled with the yarn. Their swimming abilities are very weak so they cannot break it. Ifor told me he has caught up to seven eels at a time. Personally, I think it rather hard luck on the worms.)

Various species of moss grow in the garden. In my ignorance, they seem to be of only two sorts: either little green cushions, such as those which grow on the roof or on the bark of the trees, or blankets, such as those which cover the steeper banks. The most noticeable of the latter is the blanket moss which grows in the shallower pond. This floats to the surface in early spring and then gradually sinks to the bottom as summer approaches; when the Mangrove Swamp dries up in early autumn it discloses a single carpet of the moss which is then peeled off in great sheets by the children, who use it as roofing and flooring for the huts they build from old branches.

The mosses, like the lichens, seem difficult for an amateur to identify, and sometime I will have to swot them up, or invite a more knowledgeable friend to help me list those that live in the garden.

Ferns have been more easy to identify, for we have only three ferns growing in the garden and they were named for me by a passing botanist.

She was an intense woman with a small grey moustache and a large red knapsack, and was accompanied by two churlish adolescents, one with a light moustache and a heavy scowl, the other with a brace of tiny bosoms which joggled beneath a T-shirt printed with the name of an obscure university. The botanist woman said she was doing a survey on ferns and asked if she could look through the woods on the estate, I agreed and suggested that she first should see the ones in the garden. With cries of appreciation she assented so I led her to the nearest one, a dismal little plant that sulked beneath a holly by the Near Pond. "A male fern!" she shrieked, throwing herself upon it as it if were a long-lost friend who owed her money. The next fern was in the ditch by Nut Grove. "A male fern!" she enthused, lifting up its parts in a manner that was almost lascivious. The third was on the banks of the Mangrove Swamp. She beetled up to it, bent over it, and goggled closely at it, entranced. "A male fern!" she breathed, looking up at me with wondering eyes. I could not quite understand the stamina of her enthusiasm, particularly as the moustached churl muttered to me that: "Male ferns are as common as mud," but it was heart-warming to see such repetitious rapture.

Ferns, like grasses, are often thought to be dull, but one of the most attractive stands that I have ever seen in the Chelsea Flower Show was entirely ferns, arranged, I think, by some park-keeper. The whole stand was set out like a dell, with pools fed by trickling rills, fallen timber and the occasional rock. Ferns and mosses were planted by the waterside and within the hollow tree trunks, and the total effect was one of quiet, green coolness. I was so impressed that I dug up some common polpody fern from my parents' rock garden and transplanted it among the butts and roots of two fallen oaks by the end ponds. They died, of course; it was too dark, I think.

Rose garden

CHAPTER 6

Trees

When the clay digging ceased fifty years ago, the process of natural growth immediately started on the bare soil. I have seen this happen recently in part of the Beak, which I left untilled out of curiosity. For the first couple of years agricultural weeds took over: black grass, twitch and wild oats; rest harrow, thistles and docks; then a patch or two of nettles and fireweed, followed, in the third year, by the first woody growth: briars and elder. These were later reinforced by a few hawthorns and seedlings of ash and oak. Meanwhile, from the hedge, the brambles and briars spread out and thickets of blackthorn and elm began to develop through the growth of suckers. On the banks of the small pond at the far tip of the Beak, willows began to expand and a few dogwood saplings appeared beside the apple tree which may have grown from the remnants of some farm labourer's lunch. A small gooseberry bush put in a surprise appearance.

Another surprise was the profuse amount of various types of galls, perhaps the combination of young growth together with plenty of light and open space was particularly attractive to the gall makers, which on woody plants are generally small insects of two species: the gall midges and gall wasps. When they lay their eggs in plants – often in leaf buds – they also introduce bacteria or fungi which deform the natural growth of the plant into a protective case for the eggs and young. The most noticeable of these were the robin's pin-cushions, shaggy tufts of red fibrous growth on the briars, and the oak marbles which, once they have turned brown in the autumn, are used as catapult ammunition by boys, and for

94

making necklaces by girls. This gall, now so familiar, only appeared in Britain about 1830, having been introduced here from Arabia as a dye and an ink. I also saw oak apples, about the size of small green crab-apples with a sponge-like shape, and artichoke galls which look particularly odd: the growth takes place in the leaf buds of oaks and results in a scaly excrescence like a miniature globe artichoke. I also found two types of gall on some willows, the red bean gall, which is caused by a saw fly, and another object which looked like a woody-green strawberry.

Thus, after fifty years, the basic flora in the informal part of the garden is woodland. It is of two main groups: a predominance of oak undergrown with thorn and elder in the dryer places; willow, aspen and dogwood in the damper places; the whole being bound together with a writhing tangle of briar, bramble and old man's beard, and besprinkled with examples of most of the other types of indigenous trees and shrubs: silver birches, limes, elms, ashes, maples, crab apples, hazel, privet, spindle, holly, guelder rose and wild daphne.

The noticeable absentees were alder and hornbeam, but the seed distribution of the former is greatly reliant on running water and the latter on wind dispersal, and they are too heavy to fly to the garden from the nearest hornbeam which is a stunted tree growing in the hedge half a mile away. I have introduced these two species into the Beak; it will be interesting to see if they now spread naturally.

From a distance, the most noticeable trees in the garden are the Lombardy poplars whose towering spires pierce the canopy of the other trees. There are two main groups, the line at the north end of the Back Lawn, and an avenue which borders the lane to the village. Normally these trees look aggressively un-English, but they can be forgiven for this alien appearance when we have one of those typically British twilights with a deep red sun which lowers beneath a blue-black clouded sky, and, when long, sharp shadows stretch across heavy green pastures, then the poplars catch the dying light and glow and flicker like a row of burning torches.

In general, I prefer to see trees in groves or clumps instead of single isolated specimens, perhaps because I prefer to walk amongst them, rather than stand back and look at them from a distance. Obviously a large mono-cultural collection of trees can look dreary – a fact the Forestry Commission has been slow to learn – and it is unhealthy, as too many trees of one species together can concentrate and encourage that species' own particular pests and diseases: in my own garden the groves do not exceed fifty trees of the same type.

The largest grove is the Pinetum. It is not exactly mono-cultural, being originally composed of spruce, Douglas fir, larch, western red cedar and cypresses. With few exceptions, most of these trees are ailing from the top down: the tips of the larches bend over with wind-blow or the ravages of pine moth, the spruces are dying back, and dead branches show up as brown besoms against the green of the living cypress foliage. Nevertheless the Pinetum is pleasant with its colonnades of towering trunks, and I have started to replace the dead and dying with substitutes more suited to our soil and climate. First to be planted were three sequoyas – not the Wellingtonia, which does not like chalk – but the Californian redwood, which ignores it. Wellingtonias suddenly seem to be dying all over Britain, it may be that they are fated to be short-lived in our island, and all those planted in the Wellingtonia craze during the last century have now reached their doom, but I suspect that in many cases their roots have finally struck chalk, and they are dying of disgust. Anyhow, I hope my redwoods will last the three thousand years that Nature intends them to do in the wild.

Next, for a difference in foliage, I planted an Austrian pine whose five inch needles, set in pairs, should make a pleasant and feathery contrast to the short spines of the other trees. A silver fir followed: it grows quickly, and will eventually be decorative with its smooth trunk and large cones. Finally I planted a Korean fir, an interesting tree with its hedgehog of prickles growing up each twig: its cones are possibly the most beautiful of all cones, bluish in colour with amber beads of resin, and growing when the tree is still young and only about four feet high.

I have planted some dawn redwood where the Pinetum merges with the Mangrove Swamp: it has properties suitable for both, being a damp-loving conifer. Its history is intriguing, and similar to that of the ginko; it was known to have existed about six hundred million years ago, because of its fossilised remains, but it was only discovered as a living tree in 1941, in China. Like the ginko, it loses its leaves in autumn, they change from pale green to a pinkish copper.

I have had less luck with its close relation, the swamp cypress. This also loses its leaves in autumn, but these turn bright yellow. It forms a tall, narrow spire and likes to grow out of shallow water, sending up odd protruberances from its roots, like the snouts of crocodiles, to get oxygen. Having bought one to plant in the Mangrove Swamp I then read that it dislikes chalky soils, so I dug it up and gave it to Mrs Rutland. Her soil is almost the same as mine, but her fingers are so green that, as Hart says, "I reckon she could grow marrows in a sack of coke." I knew that Brewer's Weeping Spruce has the same dislikes, but I bought one as I could not resist the description of its "long streamers of feathery branchlets, cascading down the weeping folds of its dark, mysteriously shrouded form".

The expensive little sapling that I planted by the Black Pond looked sickly after a week. I asked Hart if we could revive it in any way, but he gave it one disparaging glance and said, "It's got as much chance as a toad under a gang of harrows." He was right. It died.

The other two coniferous plantations are the groves of spruce and larch. The spruce are now dying off rapidly, as they loathe our water-logged, heavy and alkaline soil, and I have had to do some replanting. Some of this is with Lawson cypress: perhaps a rather mundane tree, but I need something to grow quickly to hide the stark outlines of the Pheasantry, and, in addition, I still want to keep a dark background for the Silver Garden. The rest of the grove has been under-planted with the wild cherry, gean; this grows very well in our locality: in one of the woods we have a vast tree which towers eighty feet with a circumference of eighty-six inches.

The larches, although ailing, are prettier than the spruces, their fluffy, light green foliage being less sombre; even the dead larches are useful, as woodpeckers like them.

Candy put two more spoonfuls of mud on my plate and then sprinkled it with pine needles.

"You're not drinking your tea," she accused Dominie who was sitting on a log next to me, holding a jam jar containing some dead leaves steeping in stagnant pond water.

"Just waiting for it to cool," her mother said tactfully. We were sitting in the drawing-room of the children's latest hut, walled with branches by George, roofed with blanket moss by Charlie and carpeted with grass mowings by Candy. Henrietta's contribution had been the occasional visit to give advice.

"She gets more like her mother every day," I said as our elder

The Silver Garden

daughter, having issued a few instructions, disappeared back towards the house.

Dominie ignored this witty thrust and said: "We've got enough conifers now, I would like to see some other types of tree which will add a bit of light to the garden, particularly birches."

I therefore decided to reinforce the 23 self-sown birches in the Silver Garden with additional birches of different species. The tallest, so far, are the paper birches which have grown over twenty feet in seven years, but their bark has not yet turned fully white, and it will be another four or five years before the pinkish-brown of their trunks has been replaced by the glossy white satins of their maturity.

The bark of the Himalayan birch will never turn white, it will remain copper coloured and peel off in strips or flakes; however, it grows up to one hundred feet in China and I am in the naive hope that it will do so here; this is unlikely as the tallest grown in Europe are around sixty feet.

The Jacqumontii is closely related to the Himalayan, but its peeling bark is more attractive, being paler, and the newer shoots of a dazzling white. The bark of the Ermanii peels in thin sheets, Bean says that the trunks are of a "creamy or pinkish white . . . the branches orange-brown".

So far, the indigenous trees are still the prettiest, particularly in snow or after an ice-storm: the delicate twigs, drooping like frozen waterfalls or swirling against the sky, can resemble the marks of frost on window panes. Although the timber is fairly useless, and rots quickly, the bark can endure for decades, the Scandinavians, for example, use it as a waterproof and durable lining for the turf-covered roofs of their cottages. I must make sure that my children do not adopt one of my own objectionable childhood activities, cutting strips of bark off birch trees to make into miniature canoes and other toys.

The area where the Silver Garden slopes down to the Near Pond was an obvious site for two types of weeping tree: Young's weeping birch and the weeping silver pear. The birch was planted on the water's edge and has proved to be interesting rather than graceful in comparison to the wild trees beside it: it looks rather dumpy and the uppermost arcs of its branches are bare of leaves. However its long, streaming rod-like branchlets look pleasant in the reflections, it becomes outstanding when caught by dew or frost and the sun glitters in the myriad of diamonds caught up amongst the hanging tresses. For some unknown reason collared doves seem to find the exposed branches of its bald scalp an attractive roosting place.

The silver weeping pear needs regular treatment because it is inclined to become a thick, tangled bush if left untended. As it grew, I cut off the lower branches to give it height; a mistake, I have just learned that the best method is to tie up a leader on a stake. I keep thinning out any twigs that, by growing towards the trunk, fill the centre: I like my weeping trees to be hollow, like umbrellas, so that I can stand inside them.

Apart from the birches, the only mono-cultural clump of self-sown trees is a grove of aspen by the Far Pond. They are curious rather than attractive at first sight, for their scraggy trunks are studded with large pointed lumps where the outer layers of bark have crawled along the twiggy remnants of dead branches, however, on looking up, one can see that the greenish-silver canopy overhead is in a constant tremor of quivering leaves and in spring thousands of long grey catkins frolic against the sky like the tails of flocks of squirrels.

Perhaps the most noticeable clump of trees is the collection of evergreens on the Back Lawn. They are mainly cypress and spruce and have an undergrowth of laurel, box and privet. I keep these shrubs trimmed, not in order to shape them in any artful fashion, but to ensure that they remain thick-set and compact. The result is that there is a greater density of nesting birds in that clump of bushes than there is anywhere else in the garden, even in the wildest and most thorny places. This is partly because of the proximity of the lawn, an attractive source of food, but I also think that an important reason may be that the birds cannot see each other amongst the heavy foliage, and thus their aggressive instincts on the subject of privacy are not aroused. Most of these nests are those of blackbird and thrush, but I have also seen, in the box only, those of chaffinch, hedge-sparrow and greenfinch.

I have never planted a tree that was not at least twenty feet tall – mostly they have towered above my head for a hundred feet – in my imagination. To me, even the meanest sapling with stunted roots and desiccated buds rears its crown amongst the clouds of the next century, and a box of sprouting acorns has the wind soughing amongst its branches. As I pack the soil around the roots of a small tree, I look forward with a mixture of resentment and pleasure to the time when my great-great-great-grandchildren will be felling it to pay for school fees. I have occasionally buried objects for them to find: a coin, or bottle or cracked kitchen mug; tomorrow's archaeological treasures.

It seems to me that in certain over-socialistic countries, where the people are not allowed to own their own houses and gardens, or in over-capitalistic ones, where employment means travelling from abode to abode in obedience to employers' whims, one sees few trees planted in gardens, because trees are planted for one's imagination and one's heirs. There are, of course, a few additional reasons for planting them: the French used to plant a grove of Lombardy poplars on the birth of a daughter in order to pay for her future dowry; lines of cypresses mantle certain unfortunate houses from the sounds of a motorway, the smells of a sewerage farm or the sight of a power station; there is the odd eccentric who really thinks he can make money by planting trees. Actually, we do make a bit out of one sort – the cricket-bat willow, which is in my opinion the only justification for a game which is as slow and as boring as chess, with the additional inconvenience of being played in a standing position.

Above all reasons, I like to see trees because they are big. I like to look up a huge old trunk and see the irregular spread of branches diminishing in perspective as they undulate towards the clouds, with crows the size of soot smuts perched against the swaying sky. A great tree makes a hollow world of its own, bounded by its screen of leaves and inhabited by its own multitude of life.

After size, shape and colour are the other attractions of trees, and many which excel in these are exotic to Britain. Thus it becomes natural to plant these more eye-catching, usually small, trees near the house, and the larger indigenous trees further away where the garden becomes wilder. A flowering magnolia often looks odd when surrounded by oaks and ashes, but alternatively there are too many houses crouching dankly beneath the shade of some prized copper beech or monkey puzzle.

As I began the replanting near the house, small exotic trees were my first introductions. I started with three which were almost instant failures. I had planted them correctly: holes were dug large enough to take the full spread of their roots; they were firmly packed about with a mixture of sand, compost and rich soil; stakes were driven into the ground before they were planted, rather than haphazardly through their roots afterwards; they were carefully watered and kept weed-free. They did not pine away, Fate dealt them thunderbolts.

The first to go was the Davidia, which was eaten by Rosie, the donkey. She had utterly ignored the thistles, nettles and brambles beside which she had been meaningfully tethered, but one day she managed to break her mooring rope, made a beeline for the Davidia lurking insignificantly beside the Boundary Hedge, and snapped it up. This was particularly peeving, for of all the trees I had read about the Davidia seemed one of the most attractive, its large white bracts, in pairs at the end of each twig, causing it to be known as the pocket handkerchief, ghost or dove tree. Later, after it had been eaten, I also read that it does not like chalky soils, so I have not replaced it.

The next to go was a wintersweet. Certain plants have special associations with one's childhood: I remember picking primroses in the local ditches when I was young enough not to worry about being thought a cissy; the fascination that I once had for the steel-blue prickle balls of the globe thistle; the lilies-of-the-valley that my Mother used to have every May Day; but above all it was the flowers of winter and early spring that I remember most, perhaps because there are so few of them at that time, or perhaps because of the wondering surprise one had at seeing snowdrops and crocuses after a winter of oblivion. In particular, the wintersweet, with its waxy, yellow and maroon flowers on the leafless twigs, and its smell which I always associate with the smell of polish in my parents' house, has been a favourite of mine. I therefore took a cutting from the old tree growing in a crinkle of my father's crinkle-crankle wall, potted it, rooted it, planted it and backed a tractor over it when pulling out some blackthorn.

The third victim was a Canadian maple. Notcutts, from whom I bought it, say its "striking fiery red foliage turns green and later golden". It barely had time to think about turning red before it was ring-barked by a rabbit.

I was more careful with my next tree, a magnolia. This was planted in the lawn in front of the front door; it is a Kobus, as this species is unlike most magnolias in liking alkaline soil. It is only just a tree rather than being a bush (the former has a single trunk, the latter several), for its branches snake out of the trunk very close to the ground. It has smallish white flowers, with narrow ribbon-like petals.

A Morello cherry was planted in the same area; dark fruit follows the profusion of flowers, but the blackbirds get much of it the day before we decide to pick, they must have some mysterious bush-telegraph about our plans. Dominie bought three Kanzan cherries and an oriental weeping cherry from Woolworths. I do not like Kanzan all that much: its pink verges on the apoplectic and it can often be seen glaring from the most inappropriate places in public parks. However, I planted them in a group to the side of the Back Lawn and I must now admit that they look attractive in flower, and have grown rapidly into fine trees.

Before we were married I gave Dominie a miniature Yorkshire terrier. When Weevil was gathered to his forefathers, an action he accomplished by eating a conker, I planted him beneath the weeping cherry, a location which combined sentiment with effective fertilisation.

As some of the Lombardy poplars along the lane were looking past their prime, I decided that, when their time was come, there would already be similar trees growing to take their place. However, I was reluctant to plant more poplars, as they last for such a short while, so I thought I would replace them with some fastigiate hornbeam. A dozen were therefore ordered but I was disconcerted to see, when they arrived, that they were fastigiate birches instead. Rather than condemn them to the rubbish pit, I planted them in a group behind the Kanzan, and now that their trunks are turning white they make an attractive tableau in the patch of grass called the Meadow Garden. I have pruned off their lower branches, for I have heard that they can become scruffily bushy if left to their own devices.

Much of my early planting concentrated on willows. The willow is not a particularly popular tree locally: when the clammy evening mists start to steam into the cold twilit air, and the shapeless, boneless things flitter and shamble after you along the ditches, when Jenny Greenteeth smiles with her dead eyes looking up through the moon-reflecting surfaces of stagnant ponds, so do the willows lean over and mumble and squeak about you as you skulk beneath. I have ignored these inconveniences and have always liked willows. In early spring, when the land is still cold and damp, the sallows flare golden amongst the leafless trees and the newly-woken

bees bumble amongst their flowers. The silver-green foliage of
white willows makes dominant patches of colour amid the all-over
effect of oak-green in my garden when seen from a distance. I have
no crack willows in the garden, but they grow along the brooks of
our land, and owls sometimes nest amidst their tormented timbers.

My first willow planting was a weeping willow by the End Pond:
perhaps too exotic a tree for such a wild and natural area, but I think
that it has managed to merge into its surroundings. Now, after
sixteen years, it is twenty feet high, and cascades of golden twigs
pour into their reflections amongst the water lilies. I later planted
weeping willows on the causeway between the Near Pond and the
Mangrove Swamp: from end-on, the avenue will eventually make a
tunnel leading past the pug mill; from the side, the direction from
which it will be seen most often, it will appear as a long barrier at the
end of the pond, and its effect will be of billowing gold in contrast to
the silver plumes of the white willows behind and to the lowering
darkness of the Pinetum to one side.

Smaller willows were planted in clumps on the banks of the Near
Pond, most of these being the types which have colourful twigs,
such as the scarlet willow – bright orange-scarlet shoots and pale
leaves – and irrorata, the shoots covered with a striking white
bloom. These usually have to be pruned each year as it is the new
growth which displays the most vivid colours, but I have let a violet
willow grow, partly out of curiosity and partly in the hope that its
sprinkling of gold pussy-willows amongst the flour-dusted purple
shoots will look attractive overhead. I will take cuttings from them
to plant around its base, and prune these for extra effect: time will
tell if the result will be superb or horrible.

Our other small-growing willows include the Wehrhahnii,
which has masses of woolly white catkins like rabbits' scuts;
Rosmarinifolia, its branches made feathery with its long narrow
leaves, and Melanostachys, very striking in early spring with its
velvety catkins which look black at first sight, but on closer
inspection show deep red glints amongst the dark fur. I took a
cutting of this from the bush of a friend while he was engrossed in
showing me his new tennis court. The fact that it only grows a few
inches a year is, perhaps, divine punishment.

I collected some willows during my visits to Scotland and
Scandinavia. Most of my cuttings came from rather dull, yard high
bushes, the least dull being the woolly willow, which has furry pale

leaves, and the Lapland willow, which has pleasant silky catkins. I stuck the twigs carefully round the pools of the Orchid Glade, and promptly forgot where I had put them. Possibly I have now removed them thinking absent-mindedly that they were part of the local regeneration, possibly some will grow to become once more identifiable in maturity.

I was given a tortuosa, which I planted on the banks of the Near Pond. It looks better without its leaves, when the weird writhing of the twigs and branches is more noticeable, but I have never liked it much since I was told, perhaps wrongly, that the tormentation is caused by a virus. I shall therefore fell it, but I shall put cuttings from it on the islands of the Mangrove Swamp to see if they, and their reflections, look better from a distance over water.

My lawns are not really large enough for specimen planting on a grand scale. When we moved in, some potentially good specimen trees existed, but they were obscured by their neighbours, and so greater emphasis was given to them by the removal of these less worthy associates. Those finally chosen as being meritorious included two Acer Pseudoplatanus one of which was crowded about by two *Malus* and a cypress; the pear which was left in the middle of the Back Lawn as sole survivor of a row; and an ordinary field maple, which was of a fine shape and size. Between this and the adjacent line of Lombardy poplars I planted three sweet chestnuts, as replacements for the poplars when they eventually fall. They will make large trees up to a hundred foot high, and are already attractive with the billowing effect of their foliage and the fizzy sprays of yellow florets. Some chestnuts, during growth, twist round so that the line marks on their trunks form curious ascending spirals. Their nuts are pleasant and seem to ripen often in this part of Britain, even though, in theory, they dislike alkaline conditions.

The particular glory of my garden trees are the two Acer Pseudoplatanus Brilliantissimum. There is no common name for them, translated, it means "most brilliant sycamore". Normally this is seen as a very small tree, as it takes so long to grow, but mine were planted nearly fifty years ago and both their height and their diameter exceed twenty feet. Like most sycamores which are allowed to grow uncrowded, they are almost perfect semi-circular domes, but their outstanding feature is their foliage which starts life in a sort of shrimp pink, then turns almost white which in its turn changes to pale cream, butter, cheese (mousetrap) and finally green;

the autumnal brown is uninteresting. One of these trees can be seen from the drawing-room, and the dark background of the Pinetum seems to make it flare out in spring like a huge glowing ball.

Although we have little room for isolated specimens, I have found a few spaces which seem reasonably appropriate. One of these was on the cleared south bank of the Near Pond. This slopes to about ten feet above the water, and I have planted a line of three weeping white limes along it. They have grown rapidly, and their leaves with downy, pale undersides flutter like small flags high above the water; a sudden surge of wind can lift up their green skirts and turn the whole line into a swirl of white petticoats. Since planting them, I have discovered that they have an unpleasant characteristic: this I learned from Elwes and Henry who wrote seven massive tomes on trees in 1906. They said that the white limes exude a poisonous narcotic from their leaves which can drug or even kill insects, and:

> in 1908, the bodies of innumerable bees, poisoned by the flowers of a tree of Tilia Petiolaris at Tortworth, had so much manured the ground under its outer branches, that a very green ring of turf was visible in the autumn following.

If this is true, then I shall fell them, but so far I have seen no evidence of this malignancy; caterpillars munch through their leaves with no apparent ill effects, and a thriving colony of red ants have piled up their hill against the trunk of the centre tree.

A space was found at the back of the Silver Garden for two Indian chestnuts after I was attracted by a description of their flowers in Bean:

> Panicles erect, cylindrical, up to 12 or even 16 inches long, white; petals 4, the upper and longer pair with a blotch of yellow and red at the base, the shorter pair flushed with pale rose; stamens standing out ¾ of an inch beyond the petals.

Like the white limes, they should reach about one hundred feet. They have fewer branches than the common conker, and their leaves are more narrow and thus do not kill the undergrowth with either a heavy summer shade or with a stifling autumn blanket. However, they can take up to fifty years to flower and meanwhile one must be content with the pleasant pinkish spring leaves.

The Larch Grove

A hedge, possibly a thousand years old, goes from the top of the woodland due east. I was rambling up it one day when I met Monk, standing morosely by a small pond. Captain Farquarson the 24th, his ferret, stared crossly and pink-eyedly at me from his jacket pocket; they seemed to be in the same mood.

"Some of your bloody tenants won't leave a single hedge on the estate, if they have their way; Wright wants to bulldoze this out and it has always been one of the best as covert." After considerable negotiations with Mr Wright I finally managed to prise the hedge, together with an adjacent strip of field, out of his tenantship. I decided to plant trees on the reclaimed land and had a most pleasant time planning what was to be planted, and where. I decided on a few hornbeam and alder, but the predominance would be oak, gean and lime. Elm would have been a natural inclusion but for the massacre of Dutch disease. I have spent much thought trying to decide what species of tree should replace the dead elms in the hedgerows on the estate. The tree would have to be a native, it would have to be tall, the growth should preferably be upwards rather than outwards for farming reasons, and it should be attractive to insects and birds. All these conditions finally narrowed the choice down to lime, not the small-leafed lime, which is inclined to be squat-trunked when in the open, nor the common lime, which grows large burrs a-bristle with twiggy growth, but the broad-leafed lime, an impressive tree which can reach 120 feet. Having made my plans for the Beak, I contacted the suppliers and found that as it was "The Year of the Tree" they had run out of everything except conifers, hornbeam and Norway maple. The latter I consider to be a drab and mundane tree: its growth is too neat and symmetrical to look appropriate in a hedgerow, and its autumn colours never reach their full potential in our climate. However, as they were the only trees available, I planted them in resentment and in rows, but these lines look pleasant enough now, as they have been broken up by their neighbours the alders and hornbeam.

I planted them as standards. We used to abide by the correct forestry practices when planting woodlands on the estate: small trees would be planted a very few feet apart and fenced against rabbits, they would be thinned out at regular intervals and sold as bean sticks, pit-props and telegraph poles, according to age; finally, after a hundred years or so, they would be sold as saw wood at a fraction of the cost of nurturing them. We now buy larger trees, plant them about ten feet apart, coil plastic anti-rabbit spirals round their stems and keep them clean from the smothering undergrowth with the use of a Jungle Buster. This is a most pleasantly destructive machine. It is towed by a tractor which pushes down the scrub in front of it with a bumper bar, the machine then rips at the prostrate growth with rows of whirling steel claws and transforms the heaps of bramble and thickets of thorn and elder into a yellow carpet of sawdust and chippings. I cannot use it in the main body of the garden as it is not manoeuvrable enough, but every other year I trundle up the three lines of trees in the Beak with very satisfactory results. I leave the expanding thicket near the woodland end, so that I can keep a record of the natural growth and as a nesting site.

I am continuing to plant trees, and I often have to restrain my impulses to plant exotic trees in the woodland part of the garden and thus ruin its wild and natural character. It has dawned on me that there are many trees and shrubs which as well as being attractive are also useful, and most of the plans I have for planting in the more formal parts of the garden now concern walnuts, mulberries, cherries and other fruit trees, but I am about to add some hollies to the evergreen clump on the Back Lawn.

Mrs Rutland told me that, before the war, some friends of hers used to get their gardeners to wash the trees, and the result was very effective on the trunks of the silver birches and yews: the latter has deep, blood-red bark which is normally smothered by a blackish-brown dust.

I therefore experimented with one of our trees; I chose a yew which was near the hose and other car-cleaning equipment, unfortunately it was also near the lane. As I soaped and scrubbed and flannelled a curious crowd began to assemble on the road, gawping at me in silent curiosity. I continued to wash away, with determined indifference, until I heard a furtive whisper: "Do you think we're on Candid Camera?" Next day the once glowing trunk looked almost as drab as it had before its bath, so I have not tried the experiment again.

"I'm afraid that this white wine is a bit warm," I apologised to a weekend guest about five winters ago.

"It must be the only thing in the house which is," he replied in what I thought an unnecessarily snide manner. These sort of remarks, together with persistent insistence from Dominie starting with "if you are too mean to pay for the central heating at least bring some logs in . . ." has resulted in a frenzy of activity every autumn. Tony Crisp, George and I get the circular saw out and for a week we cut up the windfalls and thinnings of the year for the fires of winter. We use about forty logs a day in the drawing-room alone, and much more if we have guests and have to light fires elsewhere, but so far we have managed to fuel the house almost entirely from the garden, except for a few additions from dead hedgerow elms. A friend with a wood-fired stove told me that the production of eight coppiced ash stumps, harvested on a rotational basis, should be a never-ending supply for his machine. His house is normally bitterly cold. However, we have now bought one of these stoves, and although it uses only one two-foot log per hour, it has replaced the expensive cost of five radiators in the hall.

Many of the logs are stacked indoors, and this results in the house becoming infested with insects and other invertebrates; not surprising as dead wood is the most important habitat of about twenty-percent of the fauna of a wood. I encourage insects and their ilk both for the sake of the birds that eat them and also, in certain cases, for the insects themselves: moths and butterflies are mobile flowers, the hum of bumble-bees in the springtime sallows or the chirp of crickets in a summer evening are as pleasant and as evocative as any bird-song; even an ant's hill or wasp's nest is a continuous source of fascination — and besides, one should not destroy a whole community just because one does not fancy the inhabitants.

The four dominant species of tree in the garden are particularly attractive to insects; apparently the basic rule on this subject is that the longer a tree species has been a native of an area, the more species of the local insects are liable to use it for feeding or breeding; an exception to this can be trees which are difficult to eat, such as evergreens. The number of insect species associated with most common British trees are:

284 – Oak	97 – Poplar	82 – Elm	31 – Lime
266 – Willow	93 – Apple	73 – Hazel	28 – Hornbeam
229 – Birch	91 – Scots Pine	64 – Beech	17 – Larch
149 – Hawthorn	90 – Alder	41 – Ash	7 – Holly

Encouraging invertebrates means a certain amount of untidiness. One of their most popular nursery and larder plants is the nettle, 27 species of insect are probably competely reliant on them, and one of the best suppliers of food is the hogweed. Neither of these are attractive in excess, both of them smother the prettier low-growers such as primroses and violets, however I allow three or four large patches for the sake of the insects. As dying or rotting wood is such an important resource for fauna, I stack bundles of dead twigs and branches in various unobtrusive places, and also allow a few dead trees to stand in the further reaches of the wood, because they are popular with a variety of wood-boring beetles and other insects.

The most alarming of these is the wood wasp. I first noticed this insect after hearing an assortment of yells from the kitchen. The source of the noise was Dominie, Henrietta, Candy, two stable girls, old Mrs Pipkin who comes in to bake and talk about her ailments ("So I says to the doctor, I sez, I sez to him, 'no I won't' I sez, 'I won't show you me privates, not even if you was to go on your bended knees' I sez. 'I know your sort' I sez. You could see he was disappointed cos he got reel nasty. 'Do you get off you silly old faggot,' he sez . . .") and the dogs, who had got trampled on as they slept, as usual, in front of the Aga and had got in the way of a panic-stricken rush from the windows; the cause of the excitement was a large creature that was wandering over a pane. It was bigger than a hornet and its body was brightly banded with stripes of black and yellow, but the cause of the panic was a needle on its behind, an inch long, dark and shiny. I told the assembled femininity that it was only an ovipositor and merely used for boring holes in wood in order to lay eggs, but the general opinion seemed to be that if it could bore holes in trees, it could do the same in people. I therefore removed the wasp in a jam-jar and put it on a dead larch. I have seen two other wood wasps since, so although they are said to come over in Scandinavian timber ships, I suspect that they may also breed locally.

I have not noticed many other foreign-based species of insect except for the normal influx of migrants: brimstone butterflies in the spring, "Y" moths in the autumn; the occasional plague of ladybird or hover-fly.

Most of the other insects I have noticed seem fairly mundane, though there is the occasional gaudy one which has struck the eye: the great frog-hopper, dressed in black and red, the scarlet cardinal beetle, the green tortoise beetle and, of course, the water insects such as dragonflies and diving beetles. I am still in hope of seeing my two favourites, the stag beetle and the glow-worm. Stag beetles live locally, but I am unlikely to see a glow-worm; the last one I saw was on Salisbury Plain, during an army exercise: a guardsman in my platoon was muttering in frustration as he furtively tried to light a cigarette on its phosphorescent behind.

Spiders are, to me, entirely different from insects, in that I have always loathed them. I can outstare a snake or pat a tiger, but the sight of a spider scuttling across the floor, like a hairy, disembodied hand running on its fingers, sends me zooming out of the room. Even the Orb spiders hold no charms for me, though I sometimes examine them with a sort of repelled curiosity and must admit that their dew-spangled webs, or the webs of the adolescent parachuting spiders which turn the lawn into a sheet of silver satin, both have an effect of great beauty.

Mother Nature has some revolting surprises for anyone who studies her in detail: turn the television on to a natural history programme, and you have an excellent chance of seeing Mrs Mantis eating the head off her husband, while his corpse continues to twitch in reflective sexual reaction; or hordes of ants carrying off the struggling body of a locust to their socialistic nests; or a pride (or is it humility) of hyaenas harrowing a giraffe to its death. But one does not have to go to exotic places to be repulsed by Mother Nature, the homely cabbage patch is the scene of one of her most repellent affairs.

The two participants are an Ichneumon fly and the caterpillar of the cabbage white. The common Ichneumon fly is a nasty looking creature about an inch long. It is an aggressive gingery colour; I suspect that, like others of its family, which include the wasps and ants, it can sting; it has a minutely thin waist from which is drawn a body like an elongated tear-drop. They often fly through my window when I am reading in bed, and if I slam my book shut on them their armoured bodies crunch in a series of brittle crackles.

The villain of this story, the Apechthis Rufata, is only half the size of the common Ichneumon and is black, with red legs.

The cabbage whites who dote on the Blue Bed by the swimming pool use it both for feeding and mating, and having paired, it is only necessary to flip their wings a couple of times to be over the wall and amongst the cabbages, where they lay their eggs. The resulting caterpillars are rather unattractive bloated objects dressed in an unpleasing melange of speckled greens, yellows and blacks: they rather resemble the be-stockinged legs of golfers. However, to me, they are not as revolting as the cabbages they feed on so I let them bide: Hart gives them the odd cursing and the fowls eat a few, but many escape their attention as the chickens spend most of their gastronomic time in the adjacent cornfield.

One day in early autumn I noticed hordes of these caterpillars crawling up the walls beside the chewed skeletons of the cabbages. Most of them did not reach the top, half-way up they began to slow down, stop, and then slowly writhe. I saw a brown bead appear suddenly from the flank of the caterpillar nearest me, it looked as if a minute boil had burst; this bead, a head, was followed by a tiny, maggoty body which oozed out of the dying bulk of the pupae. More and more of these grubs appeared until the caterpillar was an empty dead sack surrounded by the fuzzy yellow cocoons of its predators. This revolting scene was taking place round the bodies of most of the caterpillars on the wall.

What happens is that the female Ichneumon fly lays her eggs in the caterpillar at an early stage of its life. I have not had the misfortune to see this occur, but I have seen photographs, and for someone who gets the horrors at even the smallest tetanus injection, the sight of the wicked-looking rapier plunged up to the hilt into the passive body of the victim is enough to create shivers of sympathetic disgust.

One of the nastiest aspects is the subtlety of it: the fly does not jab her ovipositor in at random, like our local unsuccessful suicide who "keeps on puggling her ears with a hat-pin", as her lodger said, she slides it in carefully just under the skin so that the newly-born parasites will be able to start feeding on the caterpillar's fat. Having eaten this, the horrid things then nibble their way through their living meal with delicacy, studiously avoiding any vital organs until the last moment, when their host's survival is no longer of any importance to them.

I stood watching the scene and wondering why God had decided on such a revolting method of culling, and I wondered even more, a month later, when I went to inspect the Ichneumon pupae and found that most of them had been eaten by birds.

Caterpillars are often more gaudy than the resulting insects, particularly in the case of moths; and they are usually more exciting to find, as a butterfly or moth is generally noticeable from a distance, whilst the discovery of a caterpillar usually entails a thorough search. An additional interest is concerned with identification: there are plenty of books which illustrate all of the British butterflies, and several which show the moths, but I have not yet found one which shows all the caterpillars; thus the discovery of a caterpillar can often be followed by several months of frustrated curiosity.

A good example of this was an extraordinary looking creature I found lying on a half-eaten hazel leaf. It was quite large, nearly two inches, and its colour was vivid: a deep, velvety bluish-black with a hectic yellow band on each of its thirteen segments; on second sight it became even odder, for each of its segments sprouted a pair of whiskers shaped like oars: the whole effect was of a plush bolster being rowed across the surface of the leaf by thirteen little men in golden livery. My curiosity remained unanswered after I had waded through the contents of my insect books, and it was over a year before I saw and identified the moth from the caterpillar, in someone else's book: it was an alder moth. This was a bit of an anti-climax, for the moth itself turned out to be an unexciting creature dressed in an assortment of pallid greys. Most of the other exotic moth caterpillars have the similarly bathetic ending: the vapourer moth, for example, has a caterpillar which is black with red speckles and it sprouts a collection of whiskers which include, on its back, four small bunches of yellow hair looking like tiny shaving brushes – the male moth is a rather dull brown with one yellow spot on each wing, the female is wingless, and looks slightly like an unshaven slug; the extraordinary caterpillar of the lobster moth looks like the result of cross-breeding an ant with a heap of potatoes – the adult moth gives a general impression of greyish-beige; the puss moth caterpillar has an enormous clown face and two tail tubes which extrude scarlet threads – the moth is garbed in grey throughout.

A noticeable exception is the hawk moth family; although the caterpillars are quite gaudy, being large, sometimes brightly coloured and always with a noticeable spur on the tail, the moths are equally eye-catching. I bought a dozen caterpillars of the privet hawk moth, one of our largest indigenous species, and put them on some privet leaves in the wild part of the Pinetum. All but one had disappeared next day, the remaining one fattened in the same place for about a fortnight, then, one day, it was gone, in its place was a defiant and insolent replacement, a bird's mess.

I came upon Hart one day gazing morosely at the bevy of cabbage whites which fluttered about the buddleia in the Blue Garden.

"Invigorating themselves," he said sourly, "so they can lay more eggs on me cabbages." He pointed to a peacock butterfly. "When I was a boy we used to call them King Georges, I dunno which king, Edward VII was on the throne."

I have always been intrigued by Hart's knowledge of local names and, as a gull was drifting overhead, asked him what he had called them.

He brooded back over the decades in silent thought and then, as the memory came back to him, smiled nostalgically and said: "When I was a boy, all them years ago, we used to call them 'Seagulls'." Dispirited by the mundaneness of his reply, I changed the subject and asked him to keep a record of all the butterflies he saw in the garden. His resulting record, combined with mine, makes unthrilling reading: a list of common butterflies one would expect to see: plenty of whites, red admirals, peacocks, orange tips and small tortoiseshells; less commonly brimstones, commas, painted ladies, small coppers, holly and common blues; hedge and meadow browns are in profusion in the glades, the large, Essex and small skipper in the Beak. We saw several other specimens fly at treetop level, but have been unable to get close enough to identify them, they are probably purple hairstreaks: although it will look out of place in the wild garden, I have planted a buddleia there in order to attract these more elusive butterflies and thus make their identification possible.

The news sheet of the British Butterfly Conservation Society published some interesting lists, which I reproduce in appendix C, in an article by Messrs A. Newton, R. Goodden and J. Tatham, about flowers which attract butterflies.

Acer Pseudoplatanus Brilliantissimum

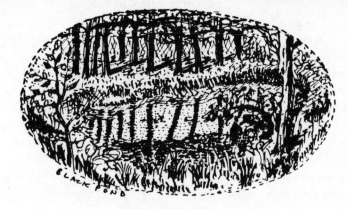

CHAPTER 7

Water

When I was a boy all the farms and cottages on my father's estate were fed by hydraulic rams and so alongside brooks and in the marshy slopes of some of the valleys one could hear the muffled thumps of the little machines working away in their underground crypts.

The hydraulic ram is one of the devices man has made closest to perpetual motion: Blakes, the manufacturers of the ones on our land, used to quote my father in their brochure saying that one of his had worked non-stop for around seventy years. The method of operation is simple, but complicated to explain, so I will merely state that the principle is based on the weight of water running into the machine and forcing part of itself (about one-eighth) up the feed pipe; the remaining water runs away on its natural course and a series of valves, together with a vacuum chamber, regulate and prepare the machine for the next pump. The basic components are a collecting tank, which gathers the water from its natural source, a downpipe leading from it to the pump – the longer the drop, the more effective the action – the pump itself, which works in a brick-built cell and the exit and feed pipes.

After the war we drilled a well over three hundred feet deep behind my father's house, and gradually the main pipe from this was extended round the estate; our pumps fell out of use, vandals threw stones into the collecting tanks and mole ploughs ripped out the piping.

Wastewood had been fed by a pump half a mile away. It was sited at the bottom of a wood, and its collecting tank was filled by a rush of clear water from an underground stream. It was one of our more recent ones, having been installed in 1943, and it fell out of use in 1955. For twenty-four years it lay forgotten. The tank silted up, the pump chamber filled with water to drown the little machine and the pipes corroded or were ploughed up.

I had always regretted that there was no running water in the garden – except during the months of heavy rains. Most people enjoy dabbling about in streams: making dams, changing courses and digging waterfalls or pools; the nearest I could get to this in the garden was to dig trenches for the occasional overflow from one pond to another. A particularly irksome occurrence was the annual drop in the water-table, every year the Mangrove Swamp dried up completely, exposing its carpet of blanket moss, and the Near Pond usually dropped at least three feet, leaving newtlets and other creatures fighting for space and oxygen in a few stagnant pools. The leaves of the water-lilies would subside into heaps like a lot of old linoleum, dead water snails would crunch underfoot; the dank smell of wet nappies would drift over the garden; the islands would lose their identities and transform into inexplicable hillocks, and willow herb and bramble seedlings would sprout up between them; the herons, kingfishers and dragonflies abandoned the Formal Garden for the End Ponds and the Muscovy ducks floated serenely, but annoyingly, on the limpid surface of the swimming pool, their naked feet wrinkling in the chlorinated water.

The only cheap answer to this was to revive the old ram, but this was not cheap enough, and the estimate for the cost of re-piping sent me boggling to the gin bottle. I therefore abandoned the idea except for the occasional wistful murmur which would start with "If we won the football pools", an unlikely occurrence, for life is too short to fill in such dreary looking forms.

On my fortieth birthday Dominie went mad with extravagance and told me that she had bought the piping for the ram as my present. After a few routine cries about her wasteful ways with money, I rushed off to discuss the subject with Bradawl, who had looked after the pumps on the estate when they were all working. The project appealed to his restorative instincts, but our mutual enthusiasm was somewhat dampened when we went to inspect the pump.

The site was in a dark hollow surrounded by sombre ashes and larches, with aged elders struggling to survive against willows and aspens, several of which had failed to hold firm in the black, marshy soil and lay tangled in decay amongst a forest of horsetails which grew too tall to see over. The earth squelched underfoot and pools of mud, liquified by springs bursting through the sides of the dell, trapped our rubber boots in clammy embraces; our faces were whipped by willows and stung by nettles as we lumbered and grappled about in search of the metal covers of the cisterns.

After several minutes I heard Bradawl call from the centre of a large elder. I ploughed through the horsetails to see what he had found: it was the well. Its rusted metal plate was firmly held down by a large stem of elder so we left it, Bradawl having marked the site by tying his handkerchief to a branch, and stumbled downhill in search of the pump.

It lay about thirty yards away, hidden in a tangle of vegetation, but its cover was reasonably clear. We gouged its sunken handles clean with twigs and prised it open. A rusting metal ladder led down to an inky square of water. The bald head of the vacuum chamber just protruded from the surface, the rest of its body was invisible in its watery grave. The occasional "plop" of a woodlouse or centipede falling off the cover into water added to the general melancholy.

Bradawl clambered cautiously down the ladder and groped about beneath the water.

"Seems all right," he said as he reappeared wiping his face dry with his wig, "I'll give it a try."

The next weekend I visited the site. It was transformed. The elder over the tank had been cut to its butt, the thirty yards between it and the pump had been cleared of all overhanging branches and rank vegetation, and neat channels had been dug to connect the over-flows to the woodside ditch. The pump chamber was dry, but empty; Bradawl had unscrewed the machine and taken it home. The cistern was full of cold, clear water, which was gushing in from the old feed pipe, twenty-three years of sediment had been cleared from it and lay on the earth beside it; it consisted of pure, coarse-grained sand.

I remembered, later, that Mr Ryan, who being a metal merchant knew such things, had told me that all running water contained minute traces of metal, including gold. I therefore took some of this sand and hopefully panned it in one of Dominie's casserole dishes: I found nothing.

The pump was apparently in excellent order. Made mainly from cast iron, gun-metal and brass, there was hardly any sign of corrosion. Bradawl told me that he had taken it to bits with surprising ease, and the only replacement necessary was a rubber washer.

Another weekend appeared, once more I went to inspect the site. The wood was quiet: most birds had felt the chill of autumn and had fallen silent. Occasionally a pigeon would clap out of the yellowing larches, or a pheasant would rustle beneath the undergrowth. Presently I became aware, out of the silence, of a quite muffled thumping, like an old heart beating underground. As I approached the pump, so the noise became louder. I lifted the cover and looked inside. With a rhythmic "gulp, snort, thump, squirt", the little machine sat at work, ignoring the inaction of the past twenty-three years. A heavy-duty polyurethane pipe was plugged into its nether end, and snaked out of the chamber towards the ditch. From it a clear stream of water poured; it tasted superb.

Several more weeks passed whilst Bradawl sorted out the best route for the pipe – a particular problem of how to get it under the road was finally solved by pushing it through a drainage pipe – trenching it in, and joining its sections together. When the first stream of water finally trickled through, Bradawl and I gazed at it like excited schoolboys. The flow was not impressive, about 720 gallons per 24 hours, but I calculated that as that represented 5,040 gallons per week, and as one gallon = .005 cubic metres, the total weekly supply of 25.2 cubic metres should cover the 435 square metreage of the pond with a depth of 5.8 cms., or 2¼ inches, not much but enough to discourage the weekly subsidence.

Thus the Near Pond should always be full of clean and oxygenated water. I will be able to have plants which cannot tolerate a periodical drying-up, such as water soldiers, and I am planning to introduce a few freshwater crayfish (for gourmandising rather than Natural Historic purposes). I had previously discovered that the introduction of fish, particularly goldfish and other bottom feeders, created clouds of mud and killed off most of the life, but I may introduce a very few Golden Orfe as they prefer to live in the top layer of water.

The other ponds, except for the Far Pond, will continue to dry out during the summer but I have managed to delay even this process.

The first method was amazingly simple, extremely satisfactory and very smelly. I discovered it by stamping on a heap of ash. This was sited in a murky hollow by the Orchid Glade: a dank, stagnant pool when full of water; a gloomy expanse of peat, dead leaves and twigs when dry; the only life which tolerated its sparse amenities seemed to be mosquito larvae, blood-worms (the little red larvae which knot and unknot their progress in old water butts, and which eventually hatch into midges), and rat-tailed maggots, unattractive grubs which live in the beds of stagnant ponds and breathe through snorkels attached to their behinds and later become drone-flies.

I had decided to encourage more life by letting in extra light on to the water, and I therefore cut away all over-hanging branches and thinned out the growth of willow, dogwood and hawthorn on its southern bank. All this brash, together with the dead twigs and branches, was piled in the middle of the dried-up pond and set alight. When I went to inspect the site at the next weekend I was surprised to see how low the heap of ash was and also to see a thin plume of smoke still wafting from the centre. I therefore strolled up to it, stamped on it, and was disconcerted to find that my leg had plunged through the heap to its full inner length. Whilst I pondered in this uncouth position – my other leg was lying at random near my head – I suddenly felt a sensation in my missing leg as if it was being baked. Hastily removing it, I looked down the hole I had made and saw it was lined with glowing embers: the peat had ignited. This was not the pleasant cake-like peat I knew in York-shire, it was a porous sponge of alternate layers of blanket moss and leaves, tied together by a motley of roots. It was impossible to dig, spades merely bounced off it, and I had therefore ignored it as a source either for fuel or for soil improvement.

For two months the peat smouldered: the air was full of the familiar, acrid smell of our Yorkshire fireplaces, and heaps of grey ash replaced the brown expanse of peat. The weather then changed and the rain pelted, beating down the ash to a half-inch-thick layer: the pond was thus about 2½ feet deeper than it had been and, in the following year, water was visible for two months longer than the previous period. After the waters had vanished in the following autumn more bonfires were built in the remaining ponds and the air once again was dense with smoke and the wheezing of bronchial birds.

When the ash had blown away or compacted on to the beds of the ponds, several things were revealed. They were firstly about the ponds themselves. I discovered that several contained deeper pits, possibly dug by the old clay workers as drainage sumps, and other ponds revealed the square-sided pans similar to those on the south edge of the Mangrove Swamp. Secondly, several objects were found. Most of these were the skeletons of moorhens and pigeons, with the occasional rabbit and the skull of a cat, but there were also several utensils and tools: broken bottles, the head of a pick, and two oddly shaped spades with very wide but shallow blades hafted with the remains of massive wooden handles. Mr Pipkin, the village builder whose firm had rented the clay yard from us fifty years before, told me that these were used to cut up the puddled clay into brick-shaped blocks.

My other method of keeping the ponds full of water was far harder work, but less pollutionary. The Far Pond is not only fed by the water table, but also by ditches and land drains from the adjacent fields. Occasionally this caused an overflow, firstly as seepage into the swampy areas of the Orchid Glade and the Willow Carr, secondly as a back-flow up two field ditches; this surplus water then soaked into the ground, some to travel beneath the surface and reappear as water table in the Near Pond and the Mangrove Swamp but most of it to flow subterraneously down the valley and into the river. I therefore dug a winding stream through the ponds of the Orchid Glade and into the expanse of the Willow Carr; from there I piped it under the drive and when the last sod was finally removed from a further thirty yards of ditch, the water gushed in a most satisfying manner into the chestnut-coloured shallows of the Mangrove Swamp. This little rill runs for six to eight weeks every spring and possibly adds a further six inches to the depth of the Mangrove Swamp. It also tops up the ponds it passes through, but it is not too deep to stop the Orchid Glade getting soggy for a certain period, thus the damp-loving plants such as sedges and fleabane continue to thrive.

When I moved into Wastewood I had the normal basic knowledge of wild plants which any countryman has, but nothing more.

During my childhood I had learned to recognise nettles, which stung, docks, whose leaves, rubbed on the rash, cured the itch and dead nettles, such as yellow archangel, which were more harmless than they looked. I recognised hogweed, whose leaves were liked as food by my pet rabbit, and ground nut, a small umbellificer which grows delicious tubers. I recognised the tall, narrow spires of agrimony, because their yellow flowers changed to burrs which could be thrown at people and stuck on their clothes, as did the burrs of burdock and goose-grass, which is why Bell and Hart called the latter "cleavers", and "sweethearts". Hips, haws, hazels, blackberries, elderberries, strawberries, crab-apples and beech-mast were pointed out as edible; in dread comparison with the berries of spindle, yew, the bryonies and nightshades. Some plants were dangerous in other ways: may was unlucky if brought in-doors, it would "sweep the head of the house away", and I remember my father getting very upset when, in all innocence, I brought some in. Sniffing poppies would make one's nose bleed, the prick from a blackthorn would always go bad.

Everyone knew primroses, violets and bluebells, though the latter were never picked as they die at once. I was rewarded with the massive sum of half-a-crown when I could identify the ten most common trees.

As time went by a little more knowledge crept in: gardeners would talk about groundsel, bell-bine and ground-elder, farmers about clover, mayweed and restharrow, Monk and other gamekeepers about buckwheat, mustard and wild privet and the local wicker-worker about the different sorts of willow, rush and reed.

Before we left Yorkshire I was given a copy of Keble Martin's reference book, *The Concise British Flora in Colour*. Since then I have been given or have bought other reference books, but I still prefer my Keble Martin, knowing my way around it and also liking its history, that of the old parson who sketched and dabbled away for sixty years in many different parishes until, when he was aged eighty-eight, his collection of drawings was finally assembled and published, the Duke of Edinburgh writing the foreword. My book is now blackened by muddy fingerprints, wrinkled by rain and torn by thorns, with a multi-coloured collection of ticks which I have marked against the names of the plants that I have found growing wild in the garden. I have not ticked introduced plants, however indigenous they may be, thus my butterburrs and alders, for example, transplanted from the river, go unacknowledged. Know-ledgeable friends have added to the number of ticks: I have also used other methods to identify the garden flora, one of the most subtle being to organise a competition, when the "Over Sixties Club" visited us, with a prize for the longest list of wild flowers seen in twenty minutes. One cunning old dear nearly won until I realised that her cow mumble, Queen Anne's lace, cow parsley, clock, dindle, piss-a-bed, dandelion, canker, gye, headache and poppy represented three plants, not eleven. Time and education are killing off all the local names, even for domesticated plants, and one is now just as likely to hear people talk of berberis as barberry, or scilla as bluebell. One of the most pleasant native names is also the longest, welcome-home-husband-however-drunk-you-may-be. The other name of this is the house-leek, the little saxifrage which grows on roofs and walls.

At first my main interest was with the rarities and, probably shamefully, I still would prefer to find a Lizard Orchid in the garden than see the whole mass of ox-eyed daisies which nod for attention in the Meadow Garden and so after I had ticked off the easily identifiable but, to me unexciting, plants such as daisies, dandelions and docks, I began to hunt about for orchids. I already knew that two types grew in the Orchid Glade, the common twayblade, which is called after its single pair of rounded leaves and which, after about fifteen years of effort, produces a spike of little green flowers – the time spent, I considered, being greatly out of proportion to the rather mundane result – and the spotted orchid, also named after its leaves, blotched with liver-coloured spots, which has pleasant spikes of pale speckled flowers, whitish in the shade, lilac to purple in the open, each flower looks rather like a minute girl wearing a gingham dress.

One day Charlie and I were standing in the Silver Garden and I told him that I would give him fifty pence if he found an orchid which was not either spotted or twaybladed. "It will probably be a bee orchid," I said, "as Mrs Simmonds said that when she was a girl before the war she and the other little girls from the village used to come to the wood here to pick them. It is quite big, about the size of a bee, and looks a bit like one, more in its shape, which has a round body with two wing-like petals rather than its colour, which is predominantly pinkish with brown markings. It is rather interesting because although it used to be pollinated by insects, it no longer is. Other orchids, such as the fly orchid, still are; they imitate female insects and are pollinated by the real males who attempt to mate with them. After a bit, it dawns on the insect that he is getting nowhere and he flies off, but stuck to the top of his head there is a sticky bead of pollen, which he transfers to another orchid during another attempt at mating with a flower. The insect that the bee orchid imitates went extinct fifty million years ago, not surprising, perhaps, if it kept wasting its ardour on something which wasn't its wife, so the flower you may see is the lonely ghost or Doppelgänger of a long-forgotten race."

After I had finished droning on, Charlie pointed between my feet: "Is this one?" he asked.

"Yes!" I screamed with excitement, and grovelling through the pages of my Keble Martin, confirmed that it really was a bee orchid. Since then, I have seen many, mostly in the Orchid Glade, growing on the mounds, but also in the Silver Garden, where my prize specimen has grown: two stems with a total of fifteen flowers. I had overlooked the orchids previously because they grew amongst grass which was covered with cuckoo-spit, and at first glance my short-sighted eyes took them to be the same.

I am not very short-sighted, just enough to make life interesting by sometimes seeing things which are not there. The best example of this was when I saw the Leprechaun in tweeds. I was leaving the house for the office at the normal vile hour of 7.15 and as I drove out of the yard I saw, on the road in front of me, a little man about a foot high. He was dressed for Newmarket Races, with a smart peaked cap of the sort known as a "Cor-blimey", a brown tweed overcoat with a herring-bone pattern, beige riding britches, tight leather boots and spurs. For a few astounded seconds I completely believed I was looking at a gnome and it was with disappointment as well as relief that I saw, when he turned sideways, that he was merely a hen pheasant.

Candy has a flower press. It was ruined almost at once because Charlie used it to press a dead dragonfly and the creature's bloated corpse buckled the layers of blotting-paper; the instrument's condition worsened when Candy used it to press her favourite flowers which grow in the garden, two wild plants which far outshine most of the exotics and highly-breds which grow in the Formal Garden: the water-lily and the flowering rush.

The huge, magnolia-like flowers of the lilies grow both in the Near and the Far Ponds. They are the ordinary wild species with waxy petals which are sometimes tinged with pink. The water-lily has a long history of association with mankind, the lotus flower was stylised in the capitals of ancient Egyptian columns; a lotus seed is one of the oldest seeds ever germinated, being over 9,000 years old.

The flowering rush – which is not a rush but the sole species of its own genus – has flowerheads which are almost globular and consist of many bright pink flowers which grow on the end of yard-high stems slightly in the same manner as ornamental onions. They seed profusely, and now that the water level is being held steady by the hydraulic ram, they are spreading from their original site in a shallow part of the Near Pond to other areas of its bank.

Another spreader is the flag iris. The bright yellow flowers are the origin of the Fleur-de-Lys, and these are followed by large brown seeds which, having broken from their pods, float to the bank and quickly take root in the ooze. I spend a great deal of time heaving the new growth out to limit it to two or three pockets in the Near Pond. I transplanted some to the Far Pond to compensate the water-fowl for the removal of the scruffy scrub in which they nested. Moorhen and dabchick, in particular, like to nest amongst its sword-like leaves. Perhaps it is these leaves which make me slightly dislike the plant, I have never liked swords since I had an accident with one when changing the guard at Buckingham Palace. During part of this ceremony, the guardsmen and non-commissioned officers stand at ease in the forecourt, the band tootles away with selections from "Salad Days", and the officers drift languorously up and down in front of the building. I was the least languorous of these officers, not only because I was usually the youngest and had to carry the Colours, but also because things always seemed to go wrong with me. On this occasion my bearskin was the cause of the trouble. Bearskins are basically wicker baskets covered in fur: the female bear is for officers (its pelt is fuzzy, and the bearskin is a few inches shorter) and in my day it was fashionable for young officers to have a slight wave in front, which attracted the girls and annoyed the adjutants. Inside, there is an arrangement made of strips of leather, a bit of string holds them together and adjusts the height so that the bottom edge of the fur is just level with one's eyes. My bit of string broke. Slowly my bearskin slipped down. My senior officers were too busy talking about the most important things in life – sex and horses – to notice the quaint figure toddling next to them, until it fell. It is a terrible thing to let the Colours drop, but their consternation at this was eliminated by their surprise at the shape of

Pollarded Willows in Near Pond

my sword – it had bent at right angles between my legs. The Drill Sergeant was summoned, a massive person who awed all ranks below Major, and with a chilly glare at me and a wrench of his wrists he straightened out my unfortunate phallic symbol.

The brigade swords are straight, the sabres of the "Donkey Wallopers" as we called the cavalry, are curved. This is the shape of the leaves of the sweet flag, but these leaves have a slight crinkle on the edge of their concave sides. They are of a paler, more yellow green than the flag iris and smell pleasantly when crushed. I had always presumed that they were the leaves that were strewn on the floors of mediaeval houses, but, although they were used for this purpose, it was not before 1596 that they were introduced to Britain. Their flower is rather dull: a thick short spike like a rhinocerous horn.

One of the prettiest water plants I have is the water plantain. There are several sorts of this, the two main ones being the common water plantain and the lanceolate water plantain. The majority of mine are the rarer lanceolate, possibly because of my fluctuating water levels: I have noticed that when the water drains from the ponds the lanceolate appear unaffected, whilst the top-heavier leaf stalks of the common water plantain snap and thus probably weaken the plant.

When they grow singly their flowers are rather insignificant, for although the white three-petalled blossoms are reasonably large – about one-third of an inch across – they grow at irregular occasions on each plant, thus only a few appear together. However, when they have formed into clumps there are more flowers and the whole effect resembles one of those fireworks which send up fountains of white sparks.

Another member of this family is the arrowhead, a tropical-looking plant whose trilobal leaves can be sharply pointed or rounded, depending, I suspect, on their age. Their flower is white with three petals, like their cousins, but has a maroon splotch in the centre and is about the size of a buttercup. I saw many of these whilst holidaying in the Midland Canals – two families of us totalling four adults, eleven children and two puppies, all crammed into a pair of old barges – and heaved them out of the mud to transplant at home. A few have survived, and as they are stoloniferous they should spread.

Another wild flower which can out-star many garden plants is

the purple loosestrife. Two clumps have rooted in shallow parts of
the Near Pond and their two foot long spikes of vivid purple
flowers sway more than six feet above the water. They are unaffected when the water table drops and exposes their roots, but if
the water cannot reach them for at least one month in a year, which
occasionally happens, they seem to grow less high and send up
fewer stems.

The giant willow-herb – fireweed – is equally tall and noticeable,
but I do not like it much, possibly because I associate it with the sad
and dreary train journeys to London just after the war, with the
fireweed growing so rampantly amongst the ruins of the East End.

The other water-side plants of note are the meadowsweet, which
has fluffy clouds of heavily scented creamy flowers, the water
forget-me-not, which makes striking blue patches of colour against
the green background of the banks, centuary, whose flowers look
like minute pink candles when they are closed for the night, and
lady's smock, also known as cuckoo pint. I got very excited over a
freak form of these, a double-flowered variety, and spent several
happy hours wondering whether to call it Dominii after my wife, or
Wastewoodii after my house. Someone then told me that these
freaks were quite common.

Mrs Rutland has a small horse pond in her garden and it grows a
large variety of flowering plants, some of which she has given to
me. She, in her turn, had scrounged many of them from other
people, like all keen gardeners she is always on the lookout for
something new, she has even stopped outside the gardens of total
strangers and wheedled cuttings from them, and she never goes to a
garden party, whether at a vicarage or at Buckingham Palace,
without a pair of secateurs.

The plants she gave me include two types of marsh marigold,
Caltha Palustris Plena, a double-flowering form, and an even larger
one whose name I cannot find. Their flowers create pleasant patches
of bright yellow on the water. I notice that their height depends on
the depth of the water in the preceding year's flowering period: if it
was deep, the flowering stems are tall, if it was shallow, the smaller
species sometimes finds itself flowering beneath the water. This
may be coincidence, but it may be some stored memory, possibly in
the roots.

The third introduction was the butterbur. Mrs Rutland had dug
several of these up from the banks of the nearby river. I transplanted

Far Pond

a few to a boggy area of the Near Pond. They disliked the move, and it was four years before the leaves attained a width of over two feet, but I have hopes that the spreading colony will finally grow leaves to their full size of three feet across. Their name originated from one of the earlier uses of these leaves: wrapping-paper for butter and cheese. Like their relation, the coltsfoot, the flowers appear before the leaves, they grow out of the ground as foot-high, conical spikes of dull, pale pink flowers.

My fourth gift from Mrs Rutland was less successful. This was the yellow water-lily, sometimes known as the brandy-bottle, according to some people this is because the shape of its seed pod resembles an old-fashioned brandy bottle, according to other people, because it smells of brandy: the second school of thought must have been educated on a fairly vile standard of alcohol. I put it in an open cardboard box which was then filled with mud and weighed down with stones and chose a shallow and sunny part of the Far Pond in which to throw it. It looked miserable the first year and was dead the next, and I suspect that it needs a certain amount of flow in the water in order to thrive.

I will try some other water-lilies, the small ornamental ones, but only in the Near Pond as they may look out of place in the wilder surroundings of the other waters.

The latest plant I have introduced to the wet areas has been an exotic: American lettuce or skunk cabbage. It looks like a large type of lords-and-ladies, but a yard high, with a hood of bright green and a fleshy white or yellow spathe, depending on the species. My plants are not growing at all, perhaps they do not like the variations in the water level.

The most noticeable water plant is the least welcome. It is not noticeable because of its flowers, a small pinkish spike, but because it rapidly covers great areas of water. It is one of the family of pond weeds, but none of my reference books identifies it exactly; it hybridises easily so is probably some sort of cross, the dominant element being floating pond weed. This pernicious plant is the aquatic equivalent of ground elder, it advances in leafy waves and even the smallest fragment of root seems to regenerate into several square feet of bronzy-greenery within a year. I prefer the main areas of my ponds to be clear of growth, with just the approved patch in selected areas: too much cover stagnates the water, kills off much of the fauna and eliminates the reflections which add extra dimensions to a pond. I thus destroy the beastly stuff whenever I have the time, except in the End Pond, where it only grows in one part and is kept at bay by an equally aggressive competitor, the water crowfoot. Blanket moss is another smotherer, but this is impossible to control without the use of chemicals, and these will kill off everything else, so I leave it alone and after a few weeks it sinks to the bottom of the pools in mid-spring.

When water weeding, it is sometimes necessary to wade up to the plant, grovel beneath the surface and haul it up by the roots. Having done this, one summer's day, I was wringing out my clothes when I suddenly heard the sound of an authoritative female voice, and on peering through the fronds of meadowsweet I spotted my great-aunt Celia: with the support of two walking sticks, a chauffeur and a female companion she was standing by the Rose Garden bellowing my name. She was neatly dressed for a formal visit, her garb including grey gloves and a black straw hat besprinkled with artificial cherries; I, on the other hand, was as naked as a worm but for my signet ring. Instantly abandoning my composure, my pile of clothes and the locality, I scuttled along the bank in a crouched position to the sanctity of a large clump of pendulous sedge.

My aunt and her entourage rootled about for a few more minutes; my dripping clothes hanging from a willow obviously intriguing them for some moments; after a few more bellows, she quit.

The fauna of the ponds varies according to their stagnancy. There are few mammals. Something lives in the the banks of Dark Pond; I have seen small burrows and have heard "plops" as their occupants dived into the water, I have even seen a speedy little swimmer below the surface, its fur coated with a silvery sheen of trapped air, like a large water beetle, but it was too fast for me to identify – it was either a bank vole or a water shrew.

The largest water animal we have is the grass snake. They can grow five feet long, but ours average two or three feet. They are, of course, harmless, and when I came upon one sloughing off its old skin I was able to squat down beside it and peer closely at its olive-green body which seemed to shine wetly in comparison to the dull grey crinkled tissue paper of its old skin; it peered back with boot-button eyes, and vibrated its black tongue angrily at me.

They are very good swimmers, undulating across the water to young moorhens or after frogs. Apparently there are more grass snakes now than there have been for centuries, and it is possible that this fact, not only the farmers' sprays and chemicals, is the cause for the shortage of frogs. In spite of ideal frog conditions, there were none in our garden when we arrived. I collected two or three from the water meadows by the river, and a year later heard the lonely cry of a bachelor frog calling for his absent mates. I expect the grass snake heard it also.

Then one day I received a parcel from Harrods which my father had ordered – he occasionally has an eccentric impulse to supply us with what he considers to be the necessities of the moment. This parcel contained a dozen floorcloths, two books, one about the friendship of a poetic cockroach and a debauched cat, the other about a man who trained his pet shark to eat his enemies, and two large tins with holes bored in their lids. I opened the first one, fifteen frogs gazed up at me; I opened the second, fifteen toads goggled likewise.

I distributed them by all the ponds and swamps in the garden: I never saw the toads again, but on occasion I have seen a few froglets in the grass. I have never found any spawn in the garden, but it sometimes appears at the same time as the blanket moss and could be difficult to discern amongst all the floating vegetation and trapped air bubbles. We often stay with friends in Dorset, and Peter kindly allows me to take home a jam jar of spawn from his moat. Similarly my brother-in-law in Norfolk lets me have some from his ditches. All these are put in one of Dominie's largest frying pans, fed with bits of weed from the ponds until they get their back legs, when they become carnivorous and can then also be fed with bacon. When they have grown their front legs they are released into the ponds; by that age they should be big enough to defend themselves from the voracity of the larvae of dragonflies and water beetles.

Locally, frogs are called "Jacobs" or "Jakies". I cannot think why, perhaps Charlie's explanation is best: the Bible says that "Jacob was a smooth man". Hart calls tadpoles "Polly-wigs" which, Charlie tells me, comes from "poll" – head – and "wriggle".

We have never been short of newts: hundreds of common newts breed in the ponds, and I sometimes see the dragon shapes of the rarer crested newts. Newts look weirdly pre-historic, tiny dinosaurs with blunt, reptilian snouts, long ridged tails and a straddle-legged walk. They seem to hibernate in the most peculiar places, and when digging away various banks by the Near Pond, I often came upon little cells, deep in the clay, containing the dark, coiled-up shapes of sleeping newts. I do not know how they got there, no burrows existed, and they looked too frail to have gouged their way through the heavy earth. They were above the water line, so no eggs could have floated through cracks in the soil: perhaps they wriggle a way in, rather like worms. Another place where they can often be discovered is in the filter baskets of the swimming pool; it is unpleasant finding them there, but not as bad as something a neighbour found in his pool filter, a six-inch long Saharan scorpion.

We have fish in the Far Pond. Thirty years ago my father put in several tench, rudd and crucian carp. These are all meant to tolerate stagnant water, but as the pond became obscured with overhanging branches and fallen trees so it became too stale for the tench and rudd; the carp which survived were small and dingy. Now that the sunlight has returned to the water, large shoals hover below the lilies and the water swirls and seethes during the spawning season.

The crucian carp is the basic ancestor of the goldfish. It rarely gets heavier than a pound, and like most carp tastes of muddy cotton wool beset with needles.

The Far Pond is meant to contain eels, but I have never seen any. Hart tells me that when it dried up early in the century they harvested two wagon loads of eels from it, but every large pond I know is rumoured to have had wagon loads of eels collected from it during droughts; wagon loads of eels are like the Indian rope trick: everyone has heard of it, no one has seen it. Similar events include the friend's friend who was struck by lightning and all the change in his pocket fused to one lump; the great aunt who met a person who knew a man who met Marie Antoinette; and the occasion when a fox plus the full pack of hounds and half the hunt ended up in a Ladies' Lavatory. (A variation of the latter is the Bank Piquet. This was the squad of guardsmen which had to march from Chelsea or Wellington Barracks every evening to guard the Bank of England. The squad consisted of about twenty guardsmen, a junior officer in front, a drummer boy at the back, holding a lantern, a sergeant at the side and a small band to lead the way. It was not allowed to stop for any reason, so one day when a squad of the Scots Guards were faced by a traffic jam at a crossroads, the officer decided that he would cunningly overcome the blockage by marching down the subway. It was, of course, a Ladies'. The cowering female occupants got their full penny's worth at the approaching sounds of skirling bagpipes and rattling drums, of thunderous marching boots and clashing bayonets and the final strident and despairing bellows of "About Turn".)

At first sight, the most obvious signs of life in the ponds are the whirligig beetles, not because of their size, as they are only as big as a peppercorn, but because they congregate together and then dance and zig-zag and twirl about each other like demented beads of mercury. Water skates are also more visible when on the move – a sudden dash across the surface of the water, their gnat-like bodies so light that they can be supported by the surface tension. This reminds me of a petulant letter I saw quoted from a newspaper several years ago. "In your last issue you said that ducks float on water because of the oil in their feathers, and if detergent was put in their pond it would wash the oil off and they would drown. I tried this and it did not happen. You can't believe a thing you read in the papers nowadays." The water-boatmen swim below the surface, looking up from their owl-like faces as their two long oars propel their orange pips of bodies upside-down. They can give a nasty nip. So, one suspects, can the larvae of the giant dragonfly and the larger diving beetles, fearsome looking monsters in armour, the latter with vast pincers like hollow hooks which pump acid into the bodies of their victims and then, when everything has liquefied, suck it back, the former with a trap-like mouth which extends like a grabbing claw and drags the victim back to the munching of the mandibles.

Some of the unfortunate victims are snails. At the Far Pond the snails are mainly wandering snails and ear pond snails, these have fewer whorls in the shell than the marsh snails which live in the Near Pond and when they die their shell can turn transparent like smokey bubbles. The ramshorn snail, which has a flat shell like the fossil of an ammonite, thrives in the Near Pond more successfully than the marsh snails until there is a drought. Their eggs do not seem to withstand drying up as well as the marsh snail, and I have had to introduce the ramshorn several times from the river. The hydraulic ram should put an end to this gloomy event. Our other notable shellfish is the swan mussel which I have already mentioned; like the snails they can dig themselves into the mud and I have seen their tracks, like furrows, which they have made as they ploughed a laborious way through the drying ooze back into the stagnant water. Their shells, up to nine inches long, are always a source of fascination to the children.

The caddis worms are not shellfish, but they build a house around their bodies, each having its own slight variation in building material: leaves and twigs, grains of sand, discarded shells, or an all-sorts of them all. They seem to hatch at the same time, like mayflies, and the surfaces of the ponds ripple in minute rings with the dipping and dancing egg-laying routine of the fluttering brown adults. Above them, hovering greedily, the hawker dragonflies manoeuvre like predatory helicopters and the metallic azure of the common blue damsel flies flash like anti-aircraft missiles.

To me, the most interesting life in the ponds is that which is the least visible; the almost microscopic mites and daphnia volvox, which swarm through every drop of water.

I saw these first in water from our well. This well is a gloomy looking shaft beside the kitchen door; it is about twenty feet deep, and only the bottom four feet holds water as it is no longer fed by the hydraulic ram, just by seepage. Bradawl lowered a jam jar on a string into its murky depths one day and drew it up full of water. Within it, tiny white specks jerked and floated, most of which, on closer inspection, proved to be minute crustaceans like the cyclops; these also live in the ponds but there they are coloured in browns and greys. More brightly coloured are the mites, some of which are tiny globes and ovals in vivid reds or greens which potter through the water with no visible method of propulsion. Some creatures move through jet propulsion, others, the infusoria for example, with rows or bunches of bristles, and a large family, the flagellata, thrash their way through the water with whiplike feelers. Some of these can be seen as swirling clouds of dancing specks in the clear depths of the water. I have tried to look at them with a microscope: Dominie gave me a beautiful brass one as a Christmas present, but I have never managed to focus this sort of instrument and usually end up squishing the object between the glass plate and the lowered lens.

A particularly interesting sight was a patch of tiny brown waving feelers on the bed of the Near Pond. I discovered them to be tubifex worms, a sort of worm which lives with its head buried in the mud and its tail undulating in the water. Scientists have recently discovered a similar sort of life several miles deep in the ocean, but there the worms are eight feet long, and have no eyes or mouth; possibly they absorb food through their skin.

one of the End Ponds

Mrs. Rutland

CHAPTER 8

'Natural' Gardening

The scope of natural gardening can range from the semi-informality of bulb plantations through to parklands, to wood or meadow gardens and up to the complete informality of a wild garden. In comparison to formal gardening the basic intention is to pretend that Mother Nature, rather than the gardener, has the dominant influence – though She usually has not – and, in certain cases, to present the local indigenous growth in as attractive a way as possible, without making it look artificial. Thus straight lines, buildings, ornaments and exotic plants are avoided, although some people allow the occasional grotto or statue.

An ancestor of mine built a hermitage in his park a couple of centuries ago; this was an unsuccessful venture as he could never find any satisfactory hermit, they either died of bronchitis or spent all their time in the kitchen, chatting up the pantry maids and guzzling themselves into unpicturesque plumpness.

Apart from the basic work of clearing and landscaping, my first essay into natural gardening was with the planting of bulbs. This was concentrated into six main areas: in front of the house, under the apple trees, in the Pinetum, beside the Silver Garden, in the rough areas of the Back Lawn and along Gnat Walk.

In all cases they had to look "natural" which meant certain principles had to be kept. Firstly, they had to be planted at random and as I have already mentioned this went completely against the grain with Bell and Hart, who doted on straight lines and circles respectively. Thus each spring I had to inspect their autumnal handiwork and break up their geometrical effects with a scattering of extra bulbs. Secondly, some bulbous plants never seem to look natural. Hyacinths and the more exotic daffodils and tulips, for example, can look as out of place and ungainly on a lawn as a parrot in a sparrow's nest. Thirdly, I think it is preferable to have large patches of similarly coloured daffodils instead of a spotty, multicoloured effect, though this seems pleasant with crocuses. And, finally, the height of the surrounding herbage is important: it is pointless, for example, to plant low autumn crocuses in a place where the grass grows high and lush and they consequently lurk unseen.

Our first effort was in the least wild of the six areas: under a clump of trees not far from the front door. I bought a "package deal" mixture of 800 crocus bulbs and with zeal and a long-handled bulb planter I began to plant. After about 100 interments the edge had gone from both zeal and bulb planter: the ground was hard, the tree roots numerous and it was difficult to keep planting at random because straight lines kept appearing as I subconsciously planted each bulb the same distance apart, about six inches. In theory, one should throw the bulbs down and plant them where they land; in practice, one loses them, stands on them, and either they all land together in huddled little clumps or yards apart, leaving large gaps.

However, next spring, all this effort was well repaid by the results: the blank patch of lawn was transformed into a shattered stained-glass window, from blues and purples which were almost iridescent, to stripes in satiny browns and lilacs and plain, clean whites and yellows.

That year the mice, sparrows and chickens were so taken aback by this blaze of colour that they left the flowers untouched, but now that they have recollected their wits it is often a race to see the flowers before they are pecked or nibbled to pieces.

In a village not far from us there is a flower gardener who specialises in selling "cut" flowers to Covent Garden. He does not actually cut them, but heaves them out of their bulbs, these, being useless for the next three years, are then thrown or given away, his only charge being a suggestion that something be contributed to his village church. I have collected about 6,000 daffodil bulbs from him, which has benefitted his church about £20, and my garden even more. All that it involves is the arrival outside his greenhouses with a trailer, the selection of boxes of bulbs, staggering out with a box under each arm (they are heavy, each one holds fifty bulbs and a load of sand), up-ending the neat, root-bound rectangles, tidily stacking the empty containers, presenting him with an envelope containing the pious contribution and then, with a bit of luck, finding someone else to do the tedious work of replanting.

Generally I choose yellow daffodils as being the most "natural", such as Golden Harvest or Unsurpassable, but I have a few other types planted in medium sized drifts of 200 or 300 bulbs, the most attractive of these being, in my opinion, a scented white narcissus with a small green eye. The sort of daffodil I cannot abide is the multiple type, such as Flower Drift, which, to me, looks like a messy and diseased mutant with its double flowers comprised of a jumble of contorted white and orange petals.

The first trailer-loads of bulbs were planted among the uncut grass beneath the apple trees, the later loads were mainly planted in the unmown areas of the Back Lawn.

Originally, I had evisaged this lawn as being one single swathe of mown grass, but Mr Codrington suggested otherwise.

Mr Codrington is a landscape gardener. His family is famous for having once reared a specially robust and healthy strain of slaves, with which they made a great deal of profit in the eighteenth century. I did not ask him to advise on our domestic service, but to get a fresh view of the garden. I thought it a good idea to get someone in who could have an unbiased look at the garden with professional and unclouded eyes. I was gratified that, in general, Mr Codrington was fairly complimentary about my efforts, and also agreed with many of my future plans. He made several useful suggestions concerning the siting of clumps of trees. Some of his advice I am leaving till a later date, but there was one suggestion he made which galvanised me into instant action, the reason being that it was so easy to execute. This was to leave certain areas of the Back Lawn uncut. It was a very pleasant job marking out the planned undulations with sticks, testing and adjusting the shape from the important vantage-points – the views from the windows of the drawing-room and my study, and from the swimming pool – and finally making the first sweeping cuts with my tractor-mower. Now, in spring, these rough patches are ablaze with daffodils and wild flowers, and the cut parts of the lawn look, in contrast, even neater. I called the largest rough patch the Meadow Garden.

Daffodils have also been planted in the Silver Garden, where their clean, cold colours match well with the trunks of the birches beside them. There I chose Magnet, a tall-growing flower with white petals surrounding a butter-yellow trumpet.

A much wider variety of bulbs and flowers was planted in the Pinetum. As the grass and weeds – such as nettles and thistles – seem to grow taller there, I have had to plant taller flowers. These included foxgloves, gladioli and giant lilies. The foxgloves were transplanted from Hadrian's Wood after a new ride had been cleared there, through the dark overhanging growth of untended Chestnut Coppice. After two years the ride had become packed with the purple spikes of fireweed, but in the third year foxgloves suddenly appeared, some of their spires thrusting up eight feet and dwarfing my children who wandered amongst them. The gladioli look similiar to their wild ancestors, Gladiolus Segetum, with a sparse row of purplish trumpets growing up a two-foot spike; it is possible that they are throwbacks from more exotic varieties planted in the garden years ago; a few years' neglect can often result in a flower "going native", hyacinths reverting into a bluebell-like flower, variegated or golden leaves becoming smothered by the more natural green growth, even potatoes trying to look like wild tomatoes.

The lilies I planted in the Pinetum were the giant lily Cardio-crinum Giganteum. According to the catalogue of Wallace and Barr, from whom I bought three very expensive bulbs:

This is the grandest, noblest, and most impressive lily of all, unique from every point of view, with enormous leaves often 16″ wide and 18″ long. The immense trumpet shaped blooms which can be as many as twenty in number thrust forward and downward around the massive stem, they are white with interior reddish purple streaks and greenish exterior.

So far, mine have not flowered, but Wallace and Barr admit, before the above-quoted effusion, that these lilies are "gross feeders", and therefore, like my brothers-in-law who, being Yorkshiremen, are similarly inclined, they may take their time.

At the east end of the Pinetum there is a clump of beech. Few plants will grow under their heavy shade, but at the edge of these shadows I have dug in some lilies-of-the-valley and cyclamen. The latter are beginning to spread, and both in spring and in autumn a pink patch suddenly glows in the darkness of the wood. These are obviously a better brought-up plant than their lily neighbours. One patch I planted elsewhere in the Pinetum has never been seen since the day I planted them; Mrs Rutland thinks I interred them all upside-down; I doubt it was mice, for if it was, the little brutes would have devoured the other patch by now.

Not even the most banal women's magazine will include a story with such stereotyped characters as the average flower catalogue: there the heroine, for example, has a "pale, wistful face, touched with a delicate flush of youthful modesty, balanced on a lithe and supple stem and dressed in a frilly ensemble of the palest green", the hero has "strong, up-thrusting limbs, a bold, regular formation and a rugged grandeur well in keeping with his lofty outlook". The villain, of course, is "weedy, intrusive, pernicious and rampant", his methods of attack being "strangling, choking and throttling", when not bent on murder he passes the time by "robbing the soil of all its nutrients".

One of the most winsome of these heroines is the snowdrop, and this is the only type of flower I have planted in Gnat Walk. I have not tried any of the more modern and exotic types – possibly they can spread as quickly as the old-fashioned sort, and possibly they can tolerate the heavy shade, but, such is the tedium of planting bulbs, I did not want to risk failure and have to do it all over again. I started at Nut Grove, where there was already a mysterious patch at the entrance of the walk: I dug some of these up, and together with others I secretly pinched during a nostalgic visit to our old Yorkshire house, I planted them in decreasing numbers towards the Far Pond, until they petered out amid the advancing hordes of primroses which were spreading down the newly cleared ground from their homes in the glades by the pond. Every year, the clumps thicken and spread and now, after six years, some of these patches look like unmelted drifts of snow dappling the winter gloom of the wood.

My latest attempt with mass bulb planting has been with bluebells. I dug up a couple of pails-full of bulbs from Hadrian's Wood – this had no effect on the millions of bulbs that I had left – and transplanted them under the oaks, ashes and willows which border the north and east of the Silver Garden. The resulting sparseness is such a pitiful echo of their original home that I will either have to plant at least twenty times as many, or wait eight hundred years.

The scope and variety of planting expanded in the Back Lawn

and the Pinetum after I read an article by Christopher Lloyd in the June and July 1976 editions of the *Royal Horticultural Society Journal* on the subject of meadow gardens. Basically he confirmed and clarified an activity that I had been doing in a somewhat dubious and half-hearted manner, namely the encouragement of selected wild flowers in certain areas, promoting them from "weeds" to "blooms"; and he added ideas which could make the result look more deliberate and less like an unkempt shambles.

A meadow garden must not be confused with a totally wild garden; in the former, flowers can be artificially introduced, in the latter, in my garden at any case, I consider it cheating to add any new plants as this will spoil the exact botanical record. The only changes are those caused by soil disturbance, which brings up dormant seeds, or by changing the micro-habitat, for example by clearing, draining or mound building which will encourage species which, though local, may have had unsuitable conditions on the site for several years. The most obvious example of this was the spread of the primroses into the cleared glades.

I had already started, in a desultory way, on meadow gardens in three areas, the uncut areas in the Back Lawn created after Mr Codrington's advice, the Silver Garden and the Pinetum; (I suppose I ought to call the latter two "woodland gardens", but the same principles apply). This work was not effected by adding plants, but by removing them: the weeds I found unsightly or in other ways unwanted. Among the ugly or uncomfortable ones I included thistles, nettles and docks; others, attractive but unwanted, included cow parsley. This is a pretty plant, and makes a pleasing white foam under the branches of the South Shrubbery, but it is very intrusive and swamps all other growth in its shade.

Much of this unwanted herbage was killed by two or three years' close mowing, a few stubborn docks and thistles got a spitefully delivered dose of weedkiller, and the cow parsley was heaved out each spring when the soil was soft. This is not particularly effective, as it does not only seed profusely, but also some of the larger roots are encircled by a ring of smaller rootlets which have sprouted directly from them and if left behind they become full-grown plants.

In the open, sunny areas of the Meadow Garden, the weeds that were allowed to thrive have a natural sequence of flowering throughout the growing season so that from April to October there are always some noticeable flowers about; in addition most of them have a strongly contrasting appearance, and often different colour, from their associates in time. There are generally at least three dominant species flowering at one time:

Stitchwort	White	April–June
Scabious	Blue/Lilac	May–June
Campion	Red	May–June
Ragged Robin	Red	May–June
Ox-eyed Daisy	White	June–August
Sowthistle	Yellow	June–August
Yarrow	White	June–August
Hypericum	Yellow	June–September
Knapweed	Purple	July–September
Poppy	Red	All summer
Mullein	Yellow	July-September
Ragwort	Yellow	July–October

In addition to these, there is a wide variety of smaller and thus less instantly noticeable plants: lords-and-ladies and dead nettles under the trees; cranesbill and speedwell in the short grass which grows in the shallow soil covering an old drive, and of course the old stagers such as buttercups, clover and dandelions. Last year, as a result of Lloyd's article, I planted some crocuses and snowdrops in areas of low grass, the small, wild-looking gladioli in the taller-growing areas, and I have at last found a tulip which looks natural in a semi-wild state, it is a Parrot Tulip with ragged, waxy petals which are basically green with creamy stripes; my father, who gave me some from his garden, has forgotten their name.

I transplanted some paigles from the hedgerows. A proper "paigle" is an oxslip, a shock-headed polyanthus whose primrose-like flowers are evenly set around the top of its stalk, but we are on the furthermost limit of the only area where this grows naturally in Britain, a few square miles covering the meeting place of Essex, Suffolk and Cambridgeshire, and to most of our locals a paigle is a cowslip, also a many-headed and slightly primrose-like plant, but with noticeably smaller and more orange-coloured flowers; these are set on one side of the stalk and all point in the same direction. I felt no guilt in digging them up, as the farmer was going to bulldoze the hedge and ditch into oblivion.

When I was a boy I used to spend a week or so each year in a castle owned by some French cousins in the Massif Central. It was a beautiful sleepy place: from my turret window I could look over the slated roofs of the little village dreaming in the soft morning air to the water meadows where yoked, slow-moving oxen pulled tumbrils through the pale blue haze of wild crocuses. In memory of this I planted a patch of wild crocus near the old pear tree, but their meagre effect does no justice to the nostalgic intention.

After Dominie had given birth to four children I suggested that we had bred enough, so in pique she started breeding ponies instead. She now has about seventy, and some of her stallions live in a pasture she has corralled off from a neighbouring field. I decided that I would merge this extra appendix with the rest of the garden. It has failed from a visual aspect: anything planted near it, from fruit trees to daffodils, has either been snapped up or trodden under, and half of the area has been fenced off and made hideous for the benefit of Henrietta and Candy with an assortment of jumps made from poles, barrels or tyres and painted in glaring colours. I have told all the children that they must learn to ride: such a skill is as necessary as swimming, shooting or bicycling, but having been learned, it need not become a habit. George and Charlie, like most boys, gave up as soon as they were allowed; Henrietta and Candy, like most girls, continued. Mr Ryan told me that it is a question of balance; males, with their large shoulders and small behinds, are top-heavy, whereas females, who are built the other way round, are by nature better built for skiing, skating, gymnastics and riding. It is only at about the age of sixteen, when boys develop their muscles, that they can begin to compete.

Ugly the pasture may be, but it is quite interesting for its wild life: it is used by lapwings, partridges, larks and other grass lovers; however, the plants are dull and verminous – ragwort, docks, thistles and mayweeds.

"You want a cow, they clean up a pasture, horses kill it," said Mr Ryan as he sipped his tea one mid-morning in the kitchen. "I like horses," said Hart indignantly. "When I was a boy I used to help the head horseman. He wore a billycock hat with a feather in it and a black and white patent-leather collar on a Sunday. Suffolks we had; Suffolks are the neatest, they stay in the furrow; Shires wander all over the place, being more slovenly."

"Pecherons are more intelligent, and Shires are more powerful," said Monk. "Mebbe," Bradawl replied, "but I've seen Suffolks set down on their knees in the heavy clay of Bell Field and pull right from the tips of their ears."

Hart chimed in dreamily: "I saw my father on his horse when I was a boy. It was at the start of the Great War and all of the cavalry was a-going to the Front. 12,000 horses were there, on parade outside Colchester, with Lancers and Hussars and Carbineers and Dragoons and Grays a-parading before the General and all their wives and kinder. And after the inspection they did a charge-past. I remember the roar and the thunder and the dust in the air and all the swords and sabres and the cuirasses a-twinkling. My father was among them. A fat lot of use his lance was to him when he went to France."

We all fell silent, moved by the glamour of this futile display. A girl-groom broke the silence. "The trouble about horses is that they're ever so strong." Mr Ryan looked at her amiably. "It's just that some people aren't as clever as they. But it's all right, me darlin', you carry a bit of bread in your armpit for a week, and give it to the horse to eat in his bait, and he'll be yours for life." Monk snickered. "She's tried that already, but young Martin Meadow-sweet still ignores her."

Hart was still in his sentimental mood. "When I was a little doddy-mite," he chanted, "we had a charm for stubborn horses. We'd get a frog and stick him on a blackthorn till he died. Then we'd burn him and chuck the ashes and bones in the reflection of a full moon in a running brook. All the bones would sink or float downstream except one; that would float upstream and that was the frog-bone. If you rubbed a horse's nose with it, he'd never go forrard, if you rubbed his arse with it, he'd pull ten ton."

Tony Crisp had remained silent throughout these tales of yore, but at last his patience snapped. Sweeping up his spanner and heavy leather gloves, and rising to go, he said; "Well, the bloody tractor has got a flat battery, so you and your bone can come along with me."

Such was the talk in the kitchen, but none of it was of much help in clearing the pasture, and so it still remains a weed-infested patch.

The further away from the house I went, the more wild the garden became. By the time I had reached the Larch Grove, I had stopped

J.C.H.   Willow Carr

planting anything and my basic aim was to encourage selected natural growth, and to allow it to be seen in the most attractive of conditions. The main way of doing this was by the creation of glades; once this had been done by the removal of the scrubby undergrowth and the felling of the more unattractive or shade-giving trees, the low-growing plants such as primroses, violets, bugle, ground ivy, and wood anemonies rapidly spread, whilst the remaining trees began to branch out in greater majesty. Even the uncleared thickets looked more attractive, as they could be viewed from a greater distance; the white froth of the flowering thorns, the golden flare of the sallows and the climbing spangles of the briars, all these were more evident, whilst on the edges of the thickets, other shrubs flowered more profusely in the improved light, particularly the dogwoods with their bunches of small, trumpet-shaped white flowers and the wild viburnum, the guelder rose, whose flat umbels of creamy flowers are followed by almost translucent red berries.

Another pleasant shrub is the daphne, or spurge laurel, one of the few indigenous woody evergreens in Britain – the others being the Scotch pine, yew, juniper, holly, box and ivy. It looks a little dull at first glance: a sprawling, low plant with the majority of its leaves growing in rosettes at the end of its branches, but it has attractive pale green flowers which are pleasantly scented.

The most successful area to be transformed is now known as the Orchid Glade. The scrub growth there was fairly sparse to start with, probably because the ground was so soggy, and I only had to remove three or four thickets of tangled thorn and dogwood, which grew on a few mounds, and clear some willow which had fallen from the edges of the small ponds. There were six of these ponds, but three were close together, so I amalgamated them into one, putting the excavated earth into the assortment of holes and hollows which pockmarked the whole area. Within two years the transformation was remarkable. The remaining growth had flourished into striking good health: where once only a few pallid spotted orchids sprouted, now little forests of lilac spires grew and another species of orchid, the twayblade, grew foot-long spikes of green flowers; flea-bane blossoms glowed like little suns, I picked some of them to put in the dog baskets to see if they really did keep away fleas; even the sedges and grasses improved and an immense variety appeared including the scarce sedge, hop sedge and false fox sedge, which grow in the damper areas, crested dogs tails and sweet vernal grass which seem to like the sunniest patches and hair grass which grows on the drier tops of mounds and ant hills. All this clearing had one irksome side effect: the growth of some invasive weeds such as nettle, cow parsley, hogweed and bramble. Certain people dote on nettles and hogweed as they are so attractive to caterpillars and insects, but I consider that they should be kept in their place and not be allowed to smother all the neighbouring growth. It is the same with brambles, which produce a pleasant berry and are good nesting sites, but they can rapidly invade any unprotected territory. They are also extremely tenacious and I have noticed that the dew berry, the shade-loving species, which has three leaves per stalk rather than five and three to five large globules of seed in its fruit, manages to survive several months' submersion in shallow ponds and also was the first growth to appear on the exposed beds of the ponds after the peat covering had been burned off. It was four years before any of these invasive plants became a nuisance, but I now find that I have to do more mowing, not just in autumn, as previously, but also once in late spring and, in certain places, also in mid-summer; this is effective with the nettles and keeps the others at bay, but only just, and I have to be careful to avoid favoured plants such as bee orchids which will not tolerate this treatment. Some woody plants are equally annoying: black-thorn and dogwood spread by suckering, and other shrubs and young trees by the edges of the newly cleared glades start to miss their previous supports and either lean out over the open space or extend new branches in the glades. All this has to be cut back. Thus "wild" gardening can take up as much time as "formal" gardening.

Wild gardening has a noticeable side effect: the increase in noise.

I remember being taught how to give lectures when I was an officer-cadet and one of the most important points, the instructor stressed, was to activate as many of the senses of the audience as possible, and I also remember the resulting tortuous attempts of some poor unfortunate who was told to stand up, and using this ruling, talk for three minutes on "A Matchstick". In fact, he did quite well: "lit and unlit, notice the difference in brightness, squad . . . you will find that one end tastes differently from the other . . . the smell, squad, depends if it comes from the cook-house stores . . . you will observe that, during ignition, it produces an interesting fizzing sound . . . feel it, does it remind you of anything, Cadet Smallbody . . ." and so on.

Almost all gardens are designed for sight alone; smell is important, but too often ignored, particularly by some breeders of fat, scentless roses; touch, except when it hurts, is also ignored – except perhaps by the Chinese (Lin Yutang wrote that half the pleasure of eating Chinese food concerns its texture rather than its taste, whether it is crisp, rubbery, crumbly, stringy, slippery or dry); taste is limited to the kitchen and herb gardeners; sound I have already mentioned when dealing with the noise of the wind through trees and bamboos. Were I Lin Yutang I suppose I would be interested in the different sorts of crunches made by walking on the various sorts of gravel paths; the noise made by water, whether falling over a cataract or dripping as condensed dew from one leaf to another and I might even have a "sound bed", so that I could compare the "click" of a vetch seed pod to the "ping" of a balsam, or run my fingers over the surface of a pig-squeak whilst popping the heads of Japanese lantern with my other hand. However, my less sophisticated English mind concentrates on birds as my main source of sound.

Being somewhat tone deaf I do not particularly concentrate on the individual "songsters", as twee people on nature programmes sometimes call them, it is the general morning twitter – the dawn chorus – that I like best, and thus the chirps of sparrows and see-saws of great tits are almost as important as the arias of blackbirds and thrushes; these prima-donnas are best in the evening, when their songs echo through the Pinetum. One song I specially like is that of the willow warbler. These olive and yellow birds live in the wild thickets further away from the house, and as I amble along Gnat Walk I am often serenaded by this very noticeable sliding-scale song. Another bird I particularly like is a late-evening singer which is active throughout the year in the evergreen clump: it sings in the summer when I am watching the evening glow of the flowers in the herbaceous borders and also in the winter, when its voice floats out of the brittle, cold darkness. I suspect it is a robin, as one of my books says that the robin's song has a "touch of quiet melancholy, reminiscent of the drifting fall of autumn leaves". Another book says it makes an assortment of "tiks", "tsips" and "ptzees", to me it merely says "tweet, tweet, tweet; twitter, twitter, tweet".

I have been told that the robin's cousin, the nightingale, has been heard in the garden, but I would probably not recognise its song which is characterised by "that marvellous crescendo on a single note, which no other birds attempt" (Warde Fowler). I used to have some ancient gramophone records on bird song, but all I learned to imitate were the ludicrously lugubrious and Germanic tones of the commentator, a Professor Ludvic Koch . . . "Ve now kome to der Trossle, vitch some peeples kall der Mizzle Trosh . . ."

I once owned a small thatched cottage in a neighbouring village, and I asked the aged incumbent if she still had her famous nightingales around her.

"Year after year them varmints kep me awake," the old dear snapped, "so one night I went out and chastised me frying pan with me rolling-pin for half an hour. I haven't heard the little buggers since," she concluded with satisfaction.

To me, no bird song can stir my spirit or raise my hackles as can the cries of the aerial damned: the wandering Jew – a golden plover – whose sudden, reluctantly heard whistle, piping down from the grey skies of winter, bodes misfortune to the hearer; or the baying of the Gabriel Ratchets, Hounds of Hell, as they hunt for lost souls amongst the clouds, it is an awesome thing to hear, as one lies amidst the safe warmness of one's pillows and blankets, this yapping and sobbing as a skein of geese flies in the night sky overhead.

One of the most impressive of bird noises is not made by a voice at all: I have not heard it often, but I have heard it in many places, from the icy solitude of an arctic tarn to the bustling busyness in the centre of London. The most dramatic occasion was at dawn as I stood on the causeway which bisects Abberton Reservoir: as the sun rose a herd of about fifty swans took off and flew over me, and their great wings sounded like windmills flailing through the air.

Of all species of birds, I think I like owls the best: they may not be more intelligent than the average bird, but they look it; their simple song appeals to my limited musical tastes; it is always with a shock of pleased surprise that one sees the great moth-like presence drifting silently past one at night. I read an article in *The Field* which stated that owls appealed to people, as did any other animal with forward-facing eyes and a round head, because they look like human babies. The chief visitors to the garden are tawny and barn owls, though we have a pair of long-eared nesting in a fir plantation nearby. Some of our visitors "churr" like nightjars, and I wonder why this odd noise seems to be a specialisation of nocturnal birds. The saddest experience we had with an owl was when we lit our drawing-room fire on the first eve of an autumn: there was a choking collection of gasps and a frantic rustling down the chimney, and then a large barn owl fell out, its great yellow eyes staring blindly from its speckled white face. It died. At least I think it did. I put the corpse in a dustbin but it was gone the next day; I presumed one of the dogs had scavenged it, but I have since heard that barn owls are masters at "playing possum", and it may have flown off with that odd chuckle I sometimes hear in the tree-tops at night.

Apart from owls, I think that I like the English partridge best: they are doting spouses, they are almost teddy-bear like in their cuddly roundness and they taste quite delicious. I ask my guests never to shoot at single pairs of English partridge, unless they are particularly good shots and are likely to kill them both. This annoys Monk. They can shoot at coveys of young birds, or at any French partridge whose married life is, as one would suspect, less blissful and more promiscuous than their British counterparts.

Partridges are said to get married on St Valentine's Day. Hart says that every year, at about that date, all the young partridges gather in the south-facing field below his house, and after a day or so of general milling about and chattering, they fly away in pairs.

It is always pleasant to walk through the Orchid Glade and suddenly flush a snipe which has been feeding in the boggy ground; it zig-zags off with a "peep" of alarm. I sometimes also see its cousin, the woodcock: one of the few birds whose eyes are positioned so that it can see behind as well as sideways and in front. I used to wonder why people kept their pin feathers as trophies, but Monk recently told me that it is because they are so fine and pointed that they are the only things suitable for portrait painters to use for the wrinkles round people's eyes. Monk believes it, anyhow. He also told me that the first Duke of Wellington used to step out of his house, No. 1, London, at Hyde Park Corner, and pot a few snipe on the banks of the Serpentine for his breakfast.

I usually see pheasants on the Back Lawn when I look out of my bedroom window in the morning. They are often joined by their close relations, the bantams, and though they peck about together in a reasonably amiable way, I notice that they often secretly stare at each other in a slightly dubious manner, like the people on either side of the enclosure at Ascot: the bantams think that the pheasants are rather smug and over-dressed, the pheasants think the bantams are too numerous and too merry.

When standing by the Far Pond I have often seen some very active little birds which take special pleasure in perching on the dragon's claw branch that I left in the water and in fluttering acrobatically after insects. They are brightly coloured with black caps and capes, and white feathers show each side of their tails as they fan them out during hovering. My bird books told me that they were reed buntings. Needless to say, they nest in reeds. Though we had plenty of sedge we had no reeds, so I went to the moat around the house of a nearby friend and pulled up some of his Norfolk reed which I transplanted into a small, shallow pool in the Orchid Glade. It is a rampant spreader and has filled the pool after two years, but has not yet invaded the dry land around it. Nor have any birds yet nested in it.

There are more thatched cottages in Essex and Suffolk than in the rest of all England, and locally we consider Norfolk reed to be by far the best material, lasting up to twice the time of the next best, wheat straw. Thatching is done in two layers, the undercoat (or waistcoat) and the overcoat. The latter, if straw, has to be changed about every fifty years, if reed, every hundred; much depends on the action of sparrows and rats. The waistcoat is changed much less often, and there are many stories of silver or weapons from the Civil War being found during this process. I do not know how true these stories are, but I did know an antique dealer in Cambridge who had found several caches of weapons in buildings. He used to tour the local villages poking and prying in the places he knew to be likely arsenals; the lofts and rafters of churches and barns. He said that he had found four big hauls in twenty years, and expected to find the odd pike or blunderbuss in about one tour in forty. In one barn he found scenes from the Battle of Waterloo painted on all the walls of the hay loft; French prisoners of war had been billeted there.

Candy loves being asked questions – preferably those to which she knows the answers. Car journeys can be made insufferably tedious by a piping and insistent voice in the back seat pleading: "Ask me the names of the most important grain crops, ask me how many ways you can roof a cottage, ask me the names of the United Arab Emirates, ask me the difference between moths and butterflies, ask me . . ." Charlie lowers the intellectual tone by interruptions such as "What is green and goes red at the touch of a button? A frog in a liquidiser. What is old and small and wrinkled and pink and belongs to Grandpapa? Grandmamma."

Candy's favourite questions are: "What are the names of Henry the Eighth's wives and what are the names of the British tits?" She then rattles off in one breath, "Katherine of Aragon Anne Boleyn Jane Seymour Anne of Cleves who he called the Flemish Mare Catherine Howard Catherine Parr Great Tit Coat Tit Blue Tit Willow Tit Marsh Tit Bottle Tit Bearded Tit Crested Tit and there's also a bird in America which is Daddy's favourite bird it's called the Tufted Tit Tyrant ask me the names of the different sort of cart horses can we stop soon I want to go to the loo I think Algy is being sick . . ."

The bearded tit (which is not a tit at all, but a babbler) and the crested tit are rare birds mainly confined, respectively to small areas of Norfolk and Speyside, but all the other six have nested in the garden: blue tits in most of the nesting boxes, great tits in the tangles of old man's beard, bottle tits in the old privet hedge, coal tits and marsh tits in holes in the lower parts of dead trees. It was several years before I found a willow tit's nest. These birds look very similar to marsh tits, the main difference being a pale patch on the willow tit's wing, their songs – the willow tit's is better and more varied – and their nesting habits: the marsh tits using existing holes in the wood, the willow tit chipping out new cases in rotting timber. Great was my pleasure in finding a small scattering of wood shavings below a huge old willow in the Mangrove Swamp and, on looking up, seeing a minute hole newly excavated in the stump of a dead branch. I lay in wait for several minutes, goggling out of a tangle of pendulous sedge, burr and bramble on the edge of the water, and finally I saw a swooping flutter of wings as the little greyish bird landed on the branch, peered about, and then sidled into the hole.

Many of the young birds seem crassly tame, the thrushes in particular: they squat on the lawn and stare at the feline approach of Pandora or Mildred with infantile curiosity, they totter up to Algy who, meeting my steely eye, sulks in baffled rage, they cheep enquiringly at me from the depths of bushes hoping that I will give them worms. Wrens, also, seem to be troublesome to their parents. The average wren family is of about five fledgelings, and once they have flown the nest they scatter like shrapnel into the nearby shrubbery, where they rustle and fidget about, apparently ignoring the frantic shepherding efforts of their parents who dash about "churring" with alarm. One summer – 1979 – the wrens seemed to be extra abundant. I spent much time digging in the Mangrove Swamp; as the waters subsided so I dug away the exposed hillocks and arranged them into four islands, thus ensuring that the main stretch of water would remain unbroken for a longer period in the following years and also creating havens where ducks could nest with less fear of foxes. As I toiled, the sallow, palm and white willow bushes beside me seethed with inquisitive wrenlets and reverberated with their parents' anxious but ineffective cries.

Later on, as the summer ended and the air of the Silver Garden shimmered with the golden fall of birch seeds, I met another delightful fledgling. It was by the waters of the Near Pond, as I stood on the bank above it, the bird merely looked up at me with affable welcome and then busily continued to pick up the birch seeds that lay stranded in the mud. It was a small bird, dressed in nondescript brown except for a natty red beret on top of its head. Hastening off to my bird books, I managed to identify it as a juvenile redpoll.

Redpolls are normally included in the flocks of small birds which congregate throughout autumn and winter. These descend on the garden in squabbling, chattering swarms and fill me with frustrated curiosity, for my combination of ignorance, short sight, deafness and slow-wittedness means that I am unable to identify half of what I see, and although I am learning, there are doubtless many buntings and finches which I have not yet recognised and recorded. The flocks of fieldfares are noticeable as the birds are large, thrush-like creatures with white flashes under their wings; I can also identify several of the gulls which silently wing overhead, high in the evening skies. Most of these skeins seem to come from the north-west, flying south-east, and often, when directly above my garden they veer further east, towards the coast: I wonder if they use us as a landmark, as we are higher than our surroundings, or if they are merely shying away from my round, pink upturned face.

A friend of mine goes every year to see the autumnal migration of birds over the Bosphorus. Several species of birds do not like flying over long stretches of the Mediterranean on their journeys between Europe and Africa or Asia, and thus the narrow gaps by the Straits of Gibraltar or the Golden Horn are settled by groups of migrants which arrive every year from all parts of the globe, even America and Australia. They congregate in large colonies on the highest points, or on the shores. The early arrivals mill about, find suitable roosts and settle to wait; a few can be observed undergoing ritual mating advances, but generally they seem merely to be conversing, and the chatter of their multitude can be heard for several miles. However, on the arrival of the first bird, they fall silent, with one accord raise their binoculars to their eyes, and remain in that position of rapt attention for about three weeks.

The birds seem to fly at different, set altitudes, the little song birds at the lowest, then hawks, then cranes and then eagles. My friend told me he counted over two thousand hawks and eagles in one hour but, magnificent though they were, they could not compare in majesty to the white sails of the slowly flapping storks and cranes.

We have a good variety of water birds, not only the moorhens, kingfishers and herons which I have already mentioned, but also duck. Mallard nest, occasionally in the Near Pond, usually in the Mangrove Swamp, always in the Far Pond; there are few prettier sights than a mallard with her dozen little ducklings, each like a large, golden bumble-bee, tacking and dabbling across the water. Little grebes have nested and I saw a pair of tufted, black and white plumaged ducks with the ability to dive and undulate through the water like seals; I do not think they nested as, though they stayed for over two months, I saw no young.

Several of our visitors have been exotics, escapees from collections, we have been visited by a muscovy, a red-crested pochard and a carolina. A pin-tailed drake may have been a domesticated bird but it may also have been a stray, when I saw it in spring it should have been busy building a nest in Scandinavia.

The ponds are too small and overhung with trees for geese and swans, they need a long stretch of water for their laborious and lengthy take-offs, but we did have a pair of swans for a week. They were found walking in a lane by the village, and the postman put them in his van and brought them to us.

"I've got some funny looking birds here," he said, flinging open the back of his van. Bell looked at the swans, then at the postman and then at me.

"He comes from Suffolk," he explained of the postman with

kindly disparagement, "he wouldn't recognise the difference between an elephant and a letter box, I shan't ask him to post my letters." He then laughed merrily at this ancient joke.

The swans were obviously tame, in spite of the ferocious scowl the cob habitually wore, and although we put them on the Far Pond they refused to live there, preferring to gaze through the glass-panelled door of the kitchen, pecking pathetically on it for food. They used to think that the letters brought by their friend the postman were slices of bread, and as they hissed and barged at his legs he had to wade through them, holding our mail above his head. They eventually left us and walked to the river.

Although the wild garden has less shrubby growth than when we moved in, it has more birds, and of a greater variety. I shall continue to make nesting sites and supply food, but also I shall continue to swot up on the subject so that I will be able to identify the results of my efforts.

The Ride Through Pinetum

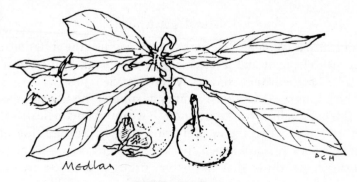

Medlar

CHAPTER 9

Food

When we were in Yorkshire and old Tod Morden, our gardener, used to spend so much of his time nurturing cabbages, I became fired by my nearly-learned art of Work Study and by my loathing of cabbages so I dogged his footsteps and eventually calculated that each cabbage cost me about ten shillings and sixpence. They cost about eight pence in the shops. This knowledge did me no good at the time as I did not dare ask him to desist from his unpleasant chore, particularly as he had become somewhat irritable and uneasy as a result of my sudden appearances from behind gooseberry bushes, with watch in one hand and notebook in the other. However, this knowledge was recalled when we moved to Wastewood: it had no Kitchen Garden and I decided not to create one. This decision met the full approval of both Bell and Hart. But as time went by, and as hosts at dinner parties proudly prattled on about the vegetables coming from their gardens, and as the prices of my special favourites increased, I began to hanker for at least a small patch where I could grow the vegetables I liked most, these, by chance, also being amongst the most expensive: Globe Artichokes and Asparagus.

My basic problem was the site. I could have compromised with the artichokes, their leaves make them acceptable as inhabitants of herbaceous borders although the real ornamental artichoke has small and prickly heads which are unsatisfactory to eat in comparison to the large heads of the edible types, but the asparagus needed a bed of its own. But where? A kitchen garden had to be near the house so that Dominie could ramble out on impulse and cut, pluck, pull or gather. It had to be in the sun which, in theory, excluded the back, north-facing side of the house, but it had to be unobtrusive, which excluded the front. To the west lay the boundary fences, to the east, the Rose Garden. Eventually I decided that, sun or not, the back of the house would have to do, just outside the kitchen window, beside Rosie's pen. I accordingly dug a large, crescent-shaped patch in the iron hard soil, lining the base with twigs and brushwood gleaned from the cleared glades. Having finished it, I paused to admire it, and instantly bell bind – devil's guts – writhed out of the soil to embrace the juvenile fuzz of grounsel and shepherd's purse. Dominie then decided that the swimming pool should be sited there, so I opted for the irregularly shaped area bought from the neighbour and laid out a series of beds. They were double-dug to start with, a job of the utmost strenuousness as the first nine inches had not been touched for four years, and so was rock hard, and the second nine inches included a layer of pan. I was interested in this pan because I had heard that it is caused by regular ploughing at a fixed depth, together with the recurring pressure of agricultural machinery, but I had never actually seen the evidence. The pan was about three inches thick and was of a slatey bluish grey; it was so hard that parts of it could be levered up like broken flagstones.

In every spit that I dug I put a load of pony manure – of which we always have an abundance – and the result has been a huge crop of artichokes, in one year they even fruited during the winter. The asparagus has fared worse, the ground gets waterlogged in winter and chickens dig around the roots in summer.

Later I decided to plant Jerusalem artichokes since, like the other two vegetables, once planted they need little attention each year except for a bit of hoeing and manuring. At school I had detested them, even more than spinach, which in those days seemed to taste like iron filings, and swedes, which were made out of ginger coloured wood-shavings and turnips which, unfortunately, tasted of turnips. I thought that my preparatory school had taught me all there was to know about vile food until I recently ate a kohlrabi. These disgusting objects look rather like dead Martians: from their globular, sickly mauve bodies weird feelers sprout and change into flipper-like leaves. They taste like turnips, but a hundred times worse. The first one I ate was at a dinner party: I took one mouthful and felt the sweat start from my forehead, whilst my stomach writhed into a knot next to my solar plexus and then jumped into my throat. I gazed in silent appeal at Dominie sitting opposite, she recognised the symptoms as the same thing happens to me when I feel a fish bone in my mouth, and replied with a withering glare of such disapproval that I gulped the whole thing down; the remainder was successfully hidden under heaps of gristle.

I finally decided to plant potatoes. Hart advised me to plant an early sort for "new" potatoes and a late sort for autumn and winter. I now grow enough to feed the whole family for half a year. They are always a bit scabby if I plant them behind the cart-lodge, this is caused by the ash left over from the old bonfires, but their taste is not affected. Hart says that completely clean potatoes can be grown by filling the trench with feathers or, slightly less effectively, with lawn mowings: everyone seems to have his own lore on the subject. The nicest thing about potatoes is digging them up, the children even volunteer to help, and enjoy scrabbling through the up-turned earth for the nuggets of buried treasure.

Some time ago I read a variety of books about bio-dynamic gardening. Most of them were written by American or German professors with uncouth names like Ppefferspitz or Stinckleblott and their styles were an odd mixture of hay-seedy innocence when discussing their pet theories and vituperative vehemence when mentioning their critics. They reminded me of certain back-to-naturists who, having spent several thousands of pounds in buying and renovating a cottage and some acres, and having thus set up a neat little capitalistic farmstead, then proceed to write scornful and testy articles about "the rat-race" and the iniquities of people who make profits.

Bio-dynamic gardening is the practice of horticulture using natural rather than artificial materials, basically fertilisers and pest-controllers. I approve of it in principle, but in practice I do not have the time to collect cigarette-ends and boil them into anti-greenfly liquors, or to hang kippers on trees to keep away bullfinches, or to brew nasturtium leaves into fly-repellents or to distill essences of nettles and comfrey into manures. My chief participation in bio-dynamic gardening is the compost heap and the bag of horse dung soaking in a vat of water.

All the books I read were fervent about compost heaps, and I amalgamated their ideas into the recipe shown in appendix E.

Our only other attempts at kitchen gardening have been Dominie's spice-bed. Below the hot, sun-reflecting south wall of the
stables she has planted a collection of herbs, only one of which
was bought, tarragon; the others came from my parents' garden
or were scrounged by me during canvassing, these include
garlic, parsley, chives, sage, and rosemary. Her other herbs are
bay, mint, lemon balm and thyme which grow in parts of the
Formal Garden, mint from the Near Pond and comfrey which
grows wild under the group of oaks and ashes by the Black
Pond.

I have been much more active with fruit trees. We took over three
lines of gnarled apples, totalling 24 trees, but they were riddled with
canker so I felled them and replaced them with a selection from
Hart's list of recommended varieties. Others from this list were
planted in the corners of the pasture: the ponies pitted their thick
wits and broad behinds against the protective fencing and finally
managed to eat half of them.

Hart, having been an orchard keeper, was obviously the right
person to ask about the correct selection of types most suitable for
our soil and climate, together with the virtues of mutual pollination, easy care, good taste and finally for variety of season. His
list may be old fashioned, but I am pleased with the result (see
appendix E again for details).

My father had planted a small cherry orchard near his house in the
hope, he said, that someone's Uncle Vanya would hang himself in
it; it also included a row of quince bushes; I dug up some of their
suckers and transplanted them beside the Near Pond. They have
flourished in the heavy boggy ground, spreading into a thicket; the
large mellow yellow fruits smell pleasantly and taste of almost
nothing, but they are good in apple pies, make an excellent chutney
and can be used in linen cupboards where their scent percolates
through the fabrics. Another old-fashioned fruit is our medlar; this
is a close relation to the rose and the hawthorn, as you can see from
its writhing branches with their random thorns, the shape of its
large white flowers and the fruit which looks like a cross between a
hip and a haw, but about the size of a golf ball. It is eaten when it is
"blet", brown and mushy after the first frosts of autumn. As a
result, not many people like it, and their repugnance is increased if
they happen to know the Elizabethan name for it: in that cheerfully
frank era medlars were called "open-arses". The taste has, with

more delicacy, been described as "subtle", a euphemism often used to magnify an insignificance.

As sloe grows well in the woodland, I presumed that domestic plums would do likewise. In addition, I had an unattractive site to the east of the pheasant house, an area made hideous after I had cleared it of growth and temporarily used it as a release pen for the birds; the ground was of very heavy and usually damp clay and Hart said that the only fruit tree which would tolerate such conditions would be the plum. I concentrated on gages, as I like them best and they seem to be becoming rare. If this primary planting succeeds, I shall plant some more and have a plum orchard. Whether the birds will allow me to have any of the fruit is less likely, but at least the trees will look pleasant and should attract interesting wild life.

Birds, and other pests, often beat me to the nuts. These I dote on, so when I found that an area of scrub to the north of the Back Lawn contained some common hazel, I left them unfelled, and in the cleared patches between them I reinforced the nut numbers with some cobs and filberts.

The nicest nuts are the purple filberts: their kernels, which look like painted finger nails, are delicious, but I thought that their puce leaves would look out of place in this area where the semi-formal garden merged with the woodland. However, on the east side of Nut Grove there is a blackthorn thicket which is very pretty in spring with the white flowers showing up against the dark wood, but some of the blackthorn are beginning to die and I am replacing them with wild bullace taken from the hedgerows. The ordinary bullace has blue damson-like fruits but the Essex bullace has golden fruit. They taste rather acrid when raw, but make a good jam.

Dominie has made jelly out of some of the ornamental crab-apples which grow in the Formal Garden, most of these jellies are of a beautiful, deep, transparent pink. Her nicest jam is hedgerow jam, the recipe being:

1 portion of hips; 1 portion of haws; 1 portion of sloes; 1 portion of rowans; 2 portions of elderberries; 2 portions of blackberries; 2 portions of crab-apples; ½ portion of hazel nuts; sugar.

Clean and de-stalk the fruit. Chop up the crab-apples. Simmer the first 4 ingredients, together with the chopped crabs, until soft (approx. 15 minutes). Sieve. Simmer all the ingredients, including the pulp and the halved nuts for 15 minutes. Add an equal measure of sugar and then boil until the jam sets. Put in hot jars.

Dominie, Candy and I picked all the ingredients in one day, except for the nuts, these had already been eaten by other scavenging animals so we had to buy some. It was very pleasing to take them to the hedges that I knew through childhood experience to be full of berries and to find that even though the memory was over thirty years old the same hedges and copses were still the best. I was seven when the war ended, so my only war contribution was picking hips for rosehip syrup, and collecting strips of silver paper off the fields: this was "Window" which aeroplanes used to drop as an anti-radar ploy.

At school I had been known as the "Caveman" because I affected a large mossy pole and built myself a variety of "huts" in the grounds; in these I used to boil trout, poached from the stream with the use of the school's tennis net, and feed them to my visitors with garnishings of boiled nettle tops, and boiled lime leaves, all washed down with tea made from boiled whitethorn buds: boiling was the only way I knew to cook. These meals made me – and my guests – realise that until recently there have been few natural plants in Northern Europe which have tasted better than their domesticated successors, as trendy as it may be to think otherwise. No wizened and sour-faced crab-apple can compare well against the most boring orchard apple, no wild member of the cabbage family tastes nearly as good as the mundane sprout or cauliflower. During the last decade, however, new developments in the mass-production of vegetables has resulted in quick-growing large-sized heaps of flavourless mush, vegetable cells pumped full of water and the resulting taste being, at best, "subtle".

I therefore began to think that we should try some of the food which grew naturally about us; nuts and some berries were already eaten, but one day I gathered a saucepan full of young nettle tops and Dominie cooked them. They tasted as I had remembered, rather like insipid spinach with the fuzzy consistency of blotting-paper. Ground elder tasted worse. I bought a book on "natural" food and, having browsed through its pages, then browsed through an assortment of roots, leaves and fungi – or intended to, but in several cases Dominie flatly refused to cook them, saying that she did not want to poison her entire family. Many were tasteless, often they were tough and stringy. The most disgusting of all seemed to be the most delicious, when I read about it. "Take a giant puff-ball, before it is fully grown," the book said, "and cut it into thin slices. Fry them in butter and serve with a white sauce." They tasted of mould; I think we ate it when it was too old.

Like most of the locals, I used to regard fungi with suspicion, suspecting all, except the mushroom, to be extremely poisonous, and considering most to be very ugly: the bracket fungi looking like bits of liver or tongues protruding from the sides of rotting timbers, the stalked ones like slimy little umbrellas. Even the fly agaric, the red toadstool with white spots, looked better in picture books, sat on by gnomes, than did the scruffy and faded examples I saw in real life.

My mother, being French, devoured an assortment of fungi which she harvested from the woods and fields during the war, but the locals considered her immunity from death was the result of having foreign innards, able to digest such things as slugs, frogs and toadstools, rather than the harmlessness of her eccentric viands.

During the war Sam and I were also made to dine on assorted oddities: moorhen's eggs, sharks, whales, pigs' faces, cocks' combs and other unmentionables shunned by the villagers; even some maggoty ham met her approval, though not mine, with her usual defence against complaints, "They're meat, and not rationed." As a result we thrived; in spite of this, our foreign ways were frowned on in the parish, particularly our eating of horsemeat: the horror which this provokes is perhaps a throwback to that time when the sacred animal, and thus the taboo, of the ancient Britons was a horse. I have wondered if this taboo is also echoed in the social convention never to call a pale horse "white", but "grey", a pure white horse once being the most sacred of the sacred animals. Perhaps the fact that fungi often grow from horse dung is also a reflection of the same ancient taboos, but this thought wanders into the realms of speculation like Robert Graves' essay in *Steps*, where he suggested that the toadstool was a Divine Object in the mind of the ancient Greeks used, for example, by the Oracles to get hallucinative inspiration, and the proof of this was the fact that the Greeks never mentioned the toadstool, a theme then taken up by someone else who wrote a long and unlikely book suggesting that Jesus was a mushroom – or Mushroom.

In spite of all these quaint speculations, my indifference to fungi persisted for many years, apart from the odd moments of pleasure caused by stamping on ripe puff-balls in order to release their clouds of spores; more amusing with the smaller, club-shaped ones such as the common puff-ball which exhale smokey jets from a hole at the top, rather than the giant puff-ball which scatters its spores in a scruffier manner, even though there are some 7,000,000,000,000,000 of them. Fairy rings could also create a glimmer of interest, not because of the toadstools which form them, but because of the necessity of having to walk round them: to step in the middle annoys the imps who use them as dance floors, and they give you gout or cramp as a punishment.

Another unpleasing feature of fungi to me was a similarity they shared with moths, being difficult to identify, either by resembling none of the illustrations in my reference books, or by having a slight resemblance to them all. However, one day, as I was walking on the high bank above the Mangrove Swamp, I noticed a colony of large, attractive toadstools. They were about eight inches high, the immature ones with round, beige heads about the size of cricket balls, attractively speckled with darker brown, the mature ones having expanded outwards and formed perfect, shield-like discs, each with a central boss. Intrigued, I bought a better reference book, *The Oxford Book of Flowerless Plants*, and discovered them to be the parasol mushroom.

With this book in hand, I now sometimes wander around the garden trying to identify the fungi I meet. I still find it difficult, particularly with some of the smaller ones which grow on the dungle next to the stables or raise minute heads above the leaf litter in the woodland, but there are some which are both easy to identify and easy to name such as the destroying angel and death-cap – the ones to learn about first, as they are the ones most often and most fatally mistaken for edible mushrooms, they have smooth, white, soft, silky skins like the hands of some trade union leaders; shaggy ink-caps – unmistakable with their tall, pointed domes covered with white scales, they liquify into a black ink, and Candy makes pretty patterns with them by dabbing them on pieces of paper; morels. They look like Martians with ridges, like veins, all over their heads, King Alfred's cakes – as their name suggests – look like charred buns.

The most intriguing of all my fungi is one that is completely invisible. It lives in the sawn-off top of a hazel stump near Spruce Grove. By daylight it cannot be seen, the level expanse of wood just shows the stains of weathering; it was at night that I first saw it. I was tip-toeing through the wood, bill-hook in one hand, Potter at my heels, thinking that I had heard Pinkhorn, the gypsy poacher. I suddenly noticed, on the hazel stump beside me, a random iridescent trail, as if a snail had wandered over the wood and left a shining track of silver behind it. Over the weeks, I inspected it several times but found no explanation. Then someone told me that certain wood-infesting fungi are phosphorescent in the dark. I now sally out on certain nights, on an impulse, to see if any of my stacks of dead timber have other glowing fungi, but I have not yet seen any.

As a result of our unsavoury experiments with eccentric "wild" foods we are now back almost entirely with the conventional mushrooms, nuts, strawberries and blackberries.

Candy occasionally contributes the filling for sandwiches: the first time that she did this was after we had to replace the floorboards of an old cottage on the estate, and I took a handful of soil beneath them which had not seen the light of day for at least two hundred years. I put it in a sterilised pan, covered it with polythene to stop any modern seeds landing on it, carefully watered it with tap water, and waited to see if any ancient or semi-extinct plants would appear, like the corncockle. My intense excitement and curiosity at the resulting thick, green growth was dampened when Candy appeared as I was puzzledly brooding over it one day. She was carrying a pair of scissors and a slice of buttered bread.

"Is the mustard and cress I planted there ready yet?" she asked.

I tried a similar experiment with some sand which I had taken off the side of a dune in the desert of Umm al Qaiwain. After I had shown the bagful to the children – they seemed irritatingly uninterested and ungrateful, considering I had brought it several thousands of miles for them to see – I asked Mrs Rutland if she would put it in a tray in her hot-house to see what happened.

Her cat used it.

I recently tried to brew some home-made wines, but this was unsuccessful. A little old woman in the village was always winning prizes for her home-made wines: elderflower and elderberry wines, parsnip wine, wine made from a blend of petals from roses, primroses and violets – they all sounded delightful but tasted of syrupy yeast mixed with cheap after-shave lotion. Under her

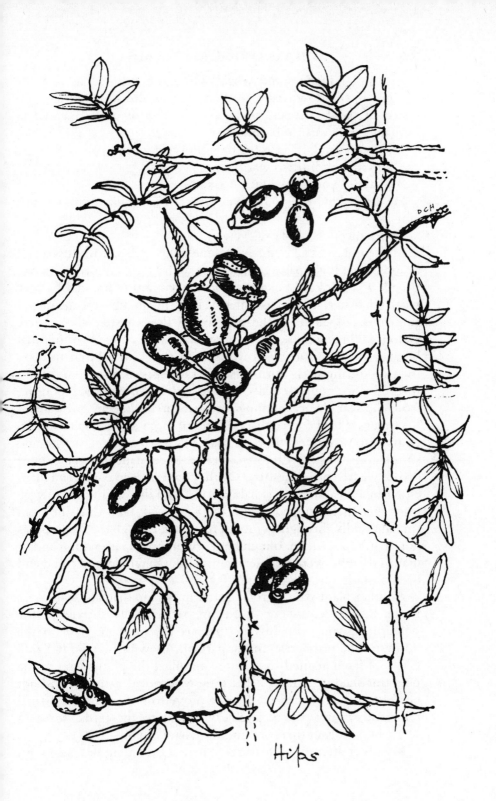

Hips

instruction I made some wheat wine, and distilled it over the radiator in the downstairs lavatory. It was almost colourless and tasted of paint stripper, so I gave the rest of it to Bradawl in exchange for some rhubarb stalks.

"Did you drink it?" I asked the following week.

"Some," he admitted warily.

"What did you think of it?" I asked.

He is a polite man, so his eyes flickered shyly like minnows in a jam-jar.

"Very nice," he said evasively.

I have not yet tried birch sap wine. This is drunk in Russia and Scandinavia. It is a pale, golden wine with a taste, according to one friend, of a smokey hock or, according to another friend, of a very weak tap water. The sap is collected in spring in the same manner as rubber is tapped from the tree, but it flows faster, about three gallons in three weeks, and the wound must be bunged up after that because the tree can bleed to death. I once cut a birch root by mistake during early spring, when the sap was rising, and for a fortnight one could actually see the ceaseless flow of sap pouring from the scar. If my attempts at silver birch wine are successful I may market it, we have several acres of birch on the estate and, in comparison to vines, they are easy to grow, cheap to attend and simple to harvest. Sycamore sap can also be made into wine, but I do not wish to plant these trees as they have little to commend them either in appearance or as habitats for wild life, and they are very intrusive, their winged seeds take root easily and thus they can spread rapidly through a wood. I read that, though the sycamore is not a native to Britain, our climatic conditions are ideal for it and, if man and rabbit were to desert our island, the whole land could end up as a single sycamore forest.

Another plant which grows better in Britain than anywhere else is the raspberry. In our Yorkshire woods they thrived in the wilderness, and with less pestiferous life in them than in the domesticated raspberries in our garden. A few grow wild in Larch Grove, I have planted some more amongst the plums next to the pheasant shed in the hope that they will spread naturally and not need too much treatment. If they prove to need attention I shall reluctantly ignore them and leave them to the birds, for as a weekend gardener there is a limit to what I can do.

My other attempt in "natural" kitchen gardening has been with wild strawberries. These, to me, are the most delicious of all fruits, though maddeningly frustrating to pick – it seems to take hours just to fill an egg cup. Elizabeth I was inordinately fond of them, but she was in the lucky position of having swarms of suitors and subjects to pick them for her. The highest and driest island in the Near Pond was covered with strawberries, so I weeded out the other plants and the island now produces a pleasant little crop every year.

Another use of wild food and herbs is as medicine. Mrs Rutland makes two home-made cures, one for coughs and the other for indigestion. She brought a bottle of the latter into the kitchen one day when she heard that Hart was there griping on about an attack of constipation:

"My innards are all of a wamble like a bag of ferrets."

She plonked the bottle on the table and immediately there was a colossal "BANG!!–––SPLATT!!" as the cork, followed by the purple contents of the bottle, hit the ceiling.

A stunned silence filled the room. It was finally broken by Hart who had been gazing uneasily at the bottle.

"Well, I see how it works," he said, "but I think I'm better."

The really pleasant thing about wild foods can be the conditions in which they are picked, either the whole family sallying out with baskets, or the solitary ramble through the woods. When Dominie is in one of her jam-making moods she organises picking ex-peditions. Last year we all set off over the burnt stubble of Bunt-ing's Field, through Hanger Wood to Too Little Field where there grows a little clump of gnarled Essex bullaces, ten old trees that are all that remains of a farm labourer's cottage. The boughs bent with the weight of the translucent, golden marbles, some clustered so thickly that it was impossible to see the twigs. While the dogs sniffled and raced around we filled the baskets and then strayed off to Sillitoe's Pasture for blackberries. As usual, all the best berries seemed just out of reach. A pony came up to me as I was stretching for a long spire-like cluster, extended its neck and neatly raked the berries off with a single delicate sweep of its massive yellow teeth. On to Bullock Dell, whilst the children mopped and mowed about the weight of the baskets, to pick elderberries and some crab-apples off a vast old tree. By this time, the total weight of the baskets was over three stone, so we put them by the field gate in Pink Stone Field, to be collected later by car, and we trailed over the darkening fields towards sunset and home.

Hart says that the two worst things for a kitchen garden are a busy housewife and a scratching hen. We have about thirty bantams, a motley crew of assorted breeds given to us by an equally motley assortment of friends. Albert and Victoria are the elders of the tribe: Hapsburgs, with rangy bodies dressed smartly for Ascot in black and white. Albert's spurs are so long that his elegance is marred by a lurching walk, each step necessitates a semi-circular movement of a spindly shank round the spur of its neighbour and occasionally, as he is standing ludicrously on one leg, the other foot seems to be groping ineffectively in the air for something to cling to and help his balance. His perambulations are further hindered by a broken toe, set permanently at right angles to the way Nature intended. The break was caused by a pony which stepped on the toe and, having stepped, stood. The normally somnambulant cock burst into furious activity, shrieking and yelling and beating his wings against the pony's leg. The pony finally shifted his foot and Albert hobbled off, cursing. Albert ruled the roost with an amiable and rather lazy vagueness until the arrival of Enoch.

Enoch was given to us by Mr Ryan because he bullied all Mr Ryan's poultry. When first seeing him, I was surprised at his aggressive reputation: he was minute, and very fat; he had a prim red face at one end, a ridiculously tiny tail at the other, and a baggy pair of plus-fours underneath, and he resembled a retired bookie who had taken up golfing. Albert took one look at him, sprang off his perch in the barn, and having chased him round the Rose Garden a couple of times, returned to his perch with a cacophony of satisfied crowings.

However, as Enoch began to feel at home, so his natural aggression became apparent: he quickly subdued Herbert, Alfred's effete son; Boris, the white Silky, was the next to be pecked into submission. Then spring came around, the hens became broody, and eventually a variety of odd-looking chicks appeared. Enoch did a most peculiar and unmasculine thing, he took a whole family under his wing. The mother was one of Albert's daughters, and like most Hapsburgs was not very maternal. Whenever Enoch found the little brood of twelve chicks wandering alone amidst the litter of the cart-lodge, cheeping dejectedly, he would sweep them around him and lead the fluffy mob to the kitchen garden, where he would assemble them into one heap and sit on them. They became devoted to him, and by the time the other chicks had abandoned their mothers, Enoch's lanky teenagers would still cluster round their foster father with admiring chirrups. Finally the young learned to fly up to the lowest rafters of the cart-lodge, and Enoch and his family would sit in a row; although each of the chicks was now about the same size as Enoch, he still insisted in covering them up for the night, and having put himself in the middle he would stretch his stumpy wings over their roosting backs. In the end he got bored with them, seduced his daughters and chastised his sons, and went off and had an affair with Mrs Gangly, a Rhode Island Red, and the only full-sized chicken in the yard. Her huge yellow feet, large angular body and continuously questing head were irresistibly attractive to the bantam cocks, and it was over her that the fateful duel was fought between Albert and Enoch.

When I came upon the scene, the battle was almost over. Both birds must have been fighting for hours in the pouring rain; they were wet, bedraggled and blood-bespattered. Poor Albert was obviously weaker, and kept tripping over his spurs; when I separated them it was Enoch who tried to continue the fight. Albert suffered great mortification for several days. No one roosted next to him in the rafters except Victoria, who remained loyal, and he skulked under a yew hedge during most of the day. However he eventually cheered up and, after giving Herbert, who had lost some respect for his better, a good thrashing, he became himself once again. Enoch is now cock of the walk, but he still regards Albert with a grudging respect, rather as Moses must have treated Rameses.

Enoch is now so tame that he walks into the kitchen, and I wrote the following in a letter to the children at school:

On mornings, Enoch comes inside,
Our breakfast crumbs intent,
On Sunday last I therefore tried
A droll experiment.
With stealth, I put a toasted crumb
On Buzz's "hinder part"
(a less rude way of saying "his bum"),
Buzz looked up with a start.
Around the region of his tail
Had he a pecking felt?

Did something like a dart impale
His furry fundament?
He looked around, he gave a glare,
But all that met his eyes
Was Enoch, standing with an air
Of innocent surprise.
So Buzz assumed a sleep-like trance
But now and then he'd send
A sudden, quick, suspicious glance
Towards our feathered friend.

As well as the bantams we have Antony, Cleopatra and Octavia, the muscovy ducks, and Ron and Eff, a pair of lilac guinea fowl who huddle about in their spotted shawls uttering a ceaseless, creaking two-note cry.

They all do the most frightful damage to the garden: they dig holes for dust baths in the beds; they eat the vegetables, and the buds off the fruit bushes; they stand with excited anticipation behind Hart when he is sowing seeds, and when he quits the spot they scrape them up and eat them; they go under the hedges to rootle about, and hurl dead leaves and twigs on to the lawn; they peck at flowers and make messes beside the swimming pool.

On the other hand, I suppose they eat slugs and wireworm and other vermin; I like to hear their voices early in the morning as they cluckle to each other outside my bedroom window, and they are much more appealing, as they toddle and gossip around the garden, than the peacocks we had for a short while for all the latters' flashy gaudiness. They even lay the occasional egg, but Dominie won't eat these as the idea of them being fertile fills her with queasiness.

My father has some ornamental ducks, and he gave us a few when we first moved into the house: a pair of mandarins – the drake has little orange sails in its back, and it grunts instead of quacks; some red-crested pochard and my favourites, two tiny chloe widgeon. Within a fortnight they had all disappeared. "A fox," said Monk, in the complacent way game-keepers have when they are able to blame their natural enemies, "if you want to keep any more you will have to net them in." This I refused to do as netting would have ruined the appearance of the Near Pond, besides, I had noticed that the ducks had stirred up the mud so that all the newts and fish had vanished in a stagnant, khaki-coloured murk. If I keep ornamental duck in the future, I shall only have a couple of pairs at the most, so that the water stays clear, and I shall choose types that roost in trees and clear of foxes, like fulvous whistling duck or carolinas.

Horse Mushrooms

Great walk

CHAPTER 10

Finale

All day, I have been in my London office: telephoning, dictating, meeting customers, giving instructions and – with habitual resentment – receiving them, lunching on a packet of peanuts and half a bottle of white wine and finally trekking home, a journey involving twenty minutes standing in the sweat-percolated underground railway, forty-seven minutes sitting in a crowded train and finishing with a fourteen mile drive along dual-carriageway, village streets and lanes.

I have thrown off my black London suit, unstrangled my tie and put on my baggy corduroys and a floppy jersey.

It is a typical summer evening as I begin my routine walk round the garden, a glass of Madeira in one hand and a sickle swinging vaguely in the other. Before me, ignoring my occasional shouts of "heel", the dogs forage and sniffle: Potter, Primmie, Bert-worm, Flopsy, Buzz and Algy. Pandora, Candy's cat, slithers beside me, mewing for attention. The dogs know the way and lead me, firstly to the cart-lodge, where they rummage for rats and mice whilst I inspect the rafters. The chickens are already roosting upon them: Albert and Victoria, an aged Darby and Joan, nestle together in the warmest and darkest corner; Enoch and five shoving and jostling wives fidget on the rungs of a ladder slung over the centre beams; the apoplectic features and white feathers of Boris glow amongst the mob of lesser breeds bunched in the northern end. All alone, the shunned figure of Herbert dejectedly rocks on a draughty outer rafter – he will have to wait before he is cock of the walk and the girls fight to cuddle up next to him. The brooding eyes of Mrs Speckled-

172

ly and Mrs Boris stare dreamily out of the nesting boxes as they warm their clutches of vari-coloured and vari-sized eggs. On the earthen floor, in a cosy gap between two bales of hay, Eff, the guinea hen, mothers her newly-hatched young, as I bend down to peer at her she gapes and hisses, and three little heads pop out of her breast feathers and stare smugly back.

We turn our backs on the cart-lodge and amble past the front of the house towards the Rose Garden, the house-martins looking down at us from their mud bowls under the eaves. Dominie must have picked some roses today, for there are some noticeable gaps and I can see, more clearly, the podgy features of the leaden statues as they glower over the bushes. A few leaves show the marks of black spot, and greenfly are beginning to amass below the flower buds: I must ask Hart to spray them next week.

We move on, between the coloured undulations of the herbaceous borders, passing through the sharp smell of camomile and the all-pervading scent of Frühlingsmorgen. Pandora stiffens in suspense as a chiff-chaff dashes out of its nest in the Lamb's Ears, so I carry her out of the way, and past the chaffinch's nest in the barberry.

I turn to walk between the avenue of newly-planted weeping willows. They are tall but straggly, and some leaves look a sickly yellow: I will have to bucket them from the pond during the weekend. Through the willows on my right I can see a moorhen scrabbling for cover over the shallow brown waters of the Mangrove Swamp; on my left, from an island in the Near Pond, a nesting mallard gazes uneasily up at us from one visible shining eye.

After I have crossed the little wooden bridge, I lie down on the pond side and stare into the busy water beneath. As my eyes focus to the microscopic range I can see that the water is teeming with minute life: little globes of green and red track across the spaces with no apparent means of locomotion; mites like tiny lobsters jerk their random ways amongst the submerged columns of rush and reed; the larvae of mosquitoes writhe through clouds of minuscule, dancing brown specks; a newt nuzzles its dragon way amongst the pillows of blanket weed, and in doing so topples over a caddis worm in its stone and twig case; with waving legs it laboriously rights itself and begins to haul up the stem of a mint; a ramshorn snail suddenly floats up from the mossy bed, gapes in a ventful of air, and slowly sinks down again; the fronds of crowfoot shake and stir and part and from them the head of a water beetle larvae protrudes, inspects its surroundings, and emerges, every section of its armoured, straddle-legged body exuding rapacious malevolence; water-skates, reassured by my immobility, start to skud across the surface, inspecting the motes that land on the water. As I stand up I can see the silver beads of whirligig beetles arabesquing amongst the shadows of the willow leaves, and a great green dragonfly hovering above the lily pads.

Many of the vetches are in flower beneath the birches of the Silver Garden: the bright yellow banana bunches of bird's foot trefoil contrasting with the long purple plumes of tufted vetch. The long twiglets of the birches sway in the slight breeze, and a tree creeper runs mouse-like up an ash trunk nearby.

The dogs race into the wheatfield on my left as I go on up Gnat Walk; they have passed a hen pheasant cowering in her nest amidst some nettles and cow-parsley: Monk says that birds lose all their scent when they are nesting.

The sliding scale of a willow-warbler's song bursts out from a hawthorn thicket, a few moments later I hear it from the top of a larch, then from the interior of a briar. Perhaps they flit about a lot, perhaps there are several birds, but it always seems to me that warblers have the power of ventriloquism.

Fortunately the dogs are still far away in the field, yapping ineffectively after a rabbit, and Pandora is sitting on my shoulders, so we arrive unheralded at the End Pond and I am able to catch a glimpse of two little tubs, dab-chicks, before they see me and quickly submerge. A pigeon claps away in alarm from its nest in the weeping willow, but a pair of collared doves, having looked up from their perch on the dragon's claw, bend down again and continue to drink. A reed-bunting and then a wagtail hover after flying insects. A swallow or house-martin – it is too fast for me to see which – zips across the surface of the pond, dips its beak in for a drink, and leaves a scar like a streak of silver on the murky water. A mosquito bites through my jersey and shirt, another lands on my cheek and a third sinks in my Madeira. I move on.

Brambles are intruding onto the footpath alongside Pregnant Pond, they creep over the ground and send long, dangling shoots down from the tangle of dogwood and blackthorn above me. My sickle lops a few of these shoots out of headway, but it will be an autumn task to get rid of them properly.

Orchid Glade

I can still hear the warbler in the distance, but now the loudest songs are those of the tits that fidget in the willows about me. Being unmusical, and forgetful of sounds, I cannot distinguish between marsh, willow, coal and blue tits; only the "see-saw" of a great tit is easy to recognise. I must ask Mrs Neild to visit us again: she says her eyes are getting bad, but she knows more with her hearing than I do with my sight.

The ground becomes soggy underfoot. I walk past a golden patch of St John's wort into the Orchid Grove. The Madeira has now been drunk by mosquito and me, so I choose a stem of sweet vernal grass to nibble. Bumble bees dither with indecision before the lilac faces of the spotted orchids, and I shove the chewed end of my grass into the green mouth of a twayblade to see it snap – as usual, it does not work. Primmie, trotting in front of me, suddenly starts back with a snort of disgust and a grass snake, with cold motionless eyes on the dog, sidles quietly into a pool. As I stand peering in, a tickling occurs about my ankles. I look down and see the mound of an ants' nest seething with activity between my feet.

Cymbeline Essex Bee and Cymbeline Esther look up from their grazing in the Paddock as I emerge from the oaks on to the drive; I blow amiably into the ponies nostrils, they blow back and wait for peppermints, but the children have already eaten them.

The hedge along the drive is beginning to look fuzzy with new shoots, but I will not be able to trim it for several weeks as it is full of nests; I hear rustling and fidgeting within as I walk along it. A flashing streak, like the flare from a Very pistol, shoots across the Mangrove Swamp, and a kingfisher disappears amongst the columns of the Pinetum.

Pandora is sitting alertly on the bench beside me. The dogs snooze, curled up, at my feet. Dusk is beginning to fall and crickets chirp in the grass of the Silver Garden. A robin – or wren – bursts into a long lullaby to its fledglings in the ivied hawthorn nearby. Bats, busy little umbrellas, flitter above the pond. The chimes of Bowers Green Church peal softly across the valley: tonight is practice night and I can hear the tenor bell of my brother Sam booming across the tintinabulation. Monk's dog barks half a mile away in its kennel, it is its dinner time. A light goes on in the window of the children's bathroom: Henrietta is getting ready for a dance. A great, white form sails moth-like from the wood, over the dew-bespangled Back Lawn, and settles on a roof ridge; a family of sparrows twitter a few sleepy curses at the unwelcome owl, and slumber back into silence. Dominie's voice calls out from the kitchen door and the dogs rush off greedily for their dinner. Two ungainly boat shapes sail into view on the pond, and Antony and Cleopatra begin to dabble amongst the flag iris and bullrushes. Another light goes on in the house and I can just hear the murmur of the children's voices.

The dusk deepens so that I can see the ox-eyed daisies glowing in the gloom. Perhaps I should plant a white-flowering bush on one of the islands . . . another tree would look pleasant in that gap in the Pinetum . . . should that bank be dug away to widen the stretch of water . . . what about a nesting box in that sallow . . . I must extend the willow avenue . . . some more ornamental grasses . . . what bird is that singing . . . ?

Dominie's voice calls out again from the kitchen door and I rush off greedily for my dinner.

Introduction & acknowledgements

In my naïvety, when I decided to keep a record of every living thing in the garden, I thought the project would be easy and would involve rambling up to the odd mole or millipede, fern or frog, and ticking their names off in my reference books. But having looked at these books in more detail I was somewhat startled to see that there are, in this country, many thousands of species of creature, as for instance: 30 indigenous mammals, 14 of which are bats; over 100 land molluscs; numerous insects including 9 bumble-bees, 30 grass-hoppers and crickets and over 5,000 flies; thousands of arthropods of which, for example, 45 are millipedes; that as far as mites, bacteria and other micro-organisms are concerned, the number living in a salt-spoonful of earth exceeds the total human population.

Several of these creatures cannot be seen without a microscope, others, such as the moths, need huge and expensive reference books for exact identification.

I also found that my Keble Martin records 1486 species of fauna, these include 2 pages of hawkweeds, all looking – to me – the same; they do not include the 400 species of the bramble family. I decided that life was too short to be spent in fiddling amongst parts of flowers with pins and tweezers, or in scrutinising the differences between bugs through a microscope. Therefore, although taking a general interest in all the flora and fauna of the garden, I have kept only a record of the basic plants, together with the mammals, birds, reptiles, amphibians, fish and butterflies, these being reasonably easy to identify. I am also recording the more noticeable of the remainder, such as some moths, spiders and molluscs.

My recording improved through a letter I wrote to Mr Joe Firmin, natural history correspondent of the Essex *County Standard*, inviting him and his associates to do any natural history survey they wished on our estate. He introduced me to Jeremy Heath, Keeper of Natural History at the Colchester and Essex Museum, to Mr Heath's assistant, Kate Hawkins, and to Alan Wake, botanical recorder of the Colchester Natural History Society. I am very grateful for their advice and information: all moths were recorded by them, and at least half of my list of flora is also due to their efforts.

Most of the leading characters in the book are founded on real people, but I have changed names, apart from those of my immediate family, because there are amalgamations or the occasional exaggeration: Monk, for example, is based on a game-keeper who has worked for us for over twenty-five years, but the odd personal characteristic or statement has been gleaned from other game-keepers I have known. I would like to thank, therefore, those people closely associated with this book who have allowed me to use them as the foundations of characters such as Hart, Monk, Mrs Rutland, Bradawl, Tony Crisp and Mr Ryan. The other people mentioned either have given their permission to be mentioned, are dead, or are imaginary.

The professional advice of Mr Barcock, Mr Codrington and the Queries Editor of *The Field* is also acknowledged with thanks.

The lists included in the appendixes also act as indexes. All these lists refer to flora and fauna actually existent in the garden. Indigenous life is mentioned with its English name first, exotic (i.e. introduced or domesticated) with its Latin name first.

I would also like to thank David Heal, who not only did the drawings, but who also, when his self-control cracked under the strain of pretending not to notice the state of the garden, would suddenly rush out of the house to do some furtive but efficient weeding.

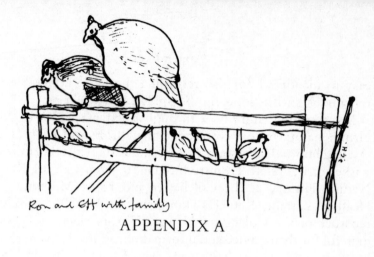

Ron and Eff with family

Fauna

At first sight, the obvious animals in the garden are the domestic ones. Most domesticated animals ruin a garden; as we have 6 dogs, 2 cats, 2 cows, about 70 ponies and an assortment of fowls, it can be seen that Dominie does not agree with this theory.

Dogs are the worst. They dig holes. They chase each other through the daffodils and flower-beds and knock everything flat. They leave repulsive messes about; to add insult to eyesore, each mess has cost about thirty pence in dog food. The urine of bitches scalds patches on lawns. In addition, each dog has its own special little vices: Algy, our Jack Russell, yaps shrilly all day down the burrows of the rabbit warren: Buzz, the Shitzu, gets his small hairy body stuck in the rose bushes: Flopsy, the Old English Sheepdog, knocks people to the ground, partly because she cannot see a thing as a mass of hair covers two minute mole-type eyes, and partly because of her amazing speed whose momentum is a disadvantage when cornering to avoid slower objects. Potter, my black labrador (known as the Black Rapist in the village, but the only dog who actually works for his keep), rubs himself along a special scratch-path on a yew hedge, uttering howls and whoops of ecstasy as he does so. His other particularly unpleasant habit is to get roots jammed across his palate. This happens when, intrigued by Algy's ceaseless yaps, he joins in the excavation of the warren. His contribution is to take great shovel-fulls of soil, like a dredger, and, in doing so, he often bites through the roots of the whitethorns which frame the cosy entrances of the burrows. These get jammed from one side to the other, and he then grovels about with both paws down his throat as if he were reaching for his tail. I then have to force him still between my knees, prise his jaws open, push my hand past his rows of glittering fangs, and grope about in the slimy hot frothiness of his throat for the offending twig; this removed, Potter condescends to wag his tail a couple of times and sniff the faggot with reproving curiosity before going back to the burrow.

Some of the more interesting mammals in the garden are merely passers-through rather than residents. Neighbouring woods harbour deer, mainly fallow, the large spotted sort with palmate horns, but also a few Chinese water deer: tiny, ugly little things about the size of a spaniel, they have tusks and their back legs are longer than their front ones, which gives the impression that they are incessantly snouting for roots. However, I have only seen the evidence for one pair of deer in the garden, slot marks in the boggy soil of Orchid Glade which Monk told me were of a fallow doe and her fawn. Similarly, I have seen no badgers but I have seen evidence that one has passed – a massive hole bored through some temporary wire netting near the Pheasantry. Like elephants, they are determined beasts and often choose to go through an obstacle rather than round it; this one was probably on its way to a set in the banks of Black Meadow, a mile away. Badgers secrete an oily yellow liquor from musk glands below their tails. This is supposed to be used as a scent marker but Monk says it is also used as food during hibernation, "They sleep," he said succinctly, "with their snouts up their arses, and sup as they sleep."

A vixen had an earth in the banks of the Far Pond during our first year, after that she de-camped, no doubt disgusted by her noisy neighbours. I have seen stoats and weasels but have found no nests. I have never liked them since I read *Wind in the Willows*: my childhood nights were often blighted by nightmares in which I fled from on-rushing hordes of vicious, sinewy bodies. I recently saw a stoat trundling a duck egg across the lane looking like a svelte, sun-tanned holiday-maker with a beach ball.

Hedgehogs live in the garden and I have found them hibernating amid the mass of dead leaves that accumulate amongst the suckering stems of hazel clumps. I leave them alone, having learned my lesson; the only hedgehog I brought indoors inflicted the house with a seething infestation of fleas. Moles, of course, abound in the garden, preferring the soft soil beside the ponds; the cats kill a few but, as with their shrew victims, never seem to eat them, just leave them to desiccate under our bed. I have heard of a man who experimented by eating every animal he could lay his teeth on, from hippopotamus to worm, and who concluded that the only animal with a really revolting taste was mole.

Like all farmsteads, we have our ineradicable quota of rats and mice; I have seen only one dormouse, not in the garden but in the lane, flat as a pancake after a meeting with a tractor.

★　　★　　★

APPENDIX B

Birds

The best way of attracting birds is to give them good nesting conditions: sites and food. The queries editor of *The Field* answered my question about owl boxes thus:

> For Tawny owl, the boxes should be vertical 30″ inside depth by 8″ square. The entrance aperture should be 8″ square, at the top of the front face there should be a lid or roof, unpitched, overlapping the box by 2″ on front and sides. The bottom of the box is best made from thin metal with six small drainage holes and a covering of fine wood shavings an inch deep. The roof should be waterproofed with roofing felt. Position, 20–40 feet up a tree substantial enough to resist wind movement, on the north side. Ensure that there are branches adjacent for the emerging fledglings to perch on. Do not attempt to disinfect before use, but clean between seasons.
>
> Barn owls require a high-entry porch in the building, preferably a triangular hole in the gable. If there is no suitable ledge inside the building, a nesting tray may be fixed. This should be 36″ × 15″ × 12″ deep with a partition 7″ high halfway along the tray. It should be positioned end-on, a few inches below the entry porch which should be made so that birds can perch in on alighting. Preferably, the hole should face neither the prevailing wind nor the light.

Since that letter Bradawl has put owl boxes up in several barns, and the occupants keep down the vermin as well as hooting pleasantly at night. Before the letter I had tried hanging orange boxes in the trees, much to the surprised gratification of grey squirrels.

For smaller birds, one can buy nesting boxes, but as squirrels take over owl boxes so, I suspect, do most manufactured bird boxes end up with infestations of squatting gnomes – some of these boxes even have little red roofs and windows painted on the walls. They are expensive, and it is cheaper and simpler to hang up old kettles, large plastic bottles or even old shoes. However, these are not frightfully ornamental and make one's garden look like a blitzed rubbish dump, so instead I make boxes very easily out of logs.

To do this one needs three tools (a hammer, brace-and-bit and saw, preferably a circular saw), some nails and, of course, the log. With these, a skilled workman could probably make a box in about two minutes by doing as follows:

1　First find your log. It should be at least a foot long by 8″ wide and preferably have its bark on. Probably some woods are better and last longer than others, but I usually use larch as it is the easiest to find in the correct proportions.

2　Cut one end off at a slope.

3　Cut a slice off at each end, about 1″ thick. (The floor and roof.)

4　Cut down four sides.

5　Discard the centre, which should be at least 4″ square.

6a　For tits: drill a hole fairly near the top, the diameter to be a twopenny bit for all tits except great tits, for these a fifty pence bit.

6b　For fly-catchers, wrens, robins, etc.: saw the top third off one of the sides.

7　Nail the four sides and the floor back to their original positions.

8　Optional. Stick a perch on, a peg of wood is better than a nail. I do not bother, as I place the boxes near twigs conveniently close for the birds to perch.

9　Put the roof on (the bit with the slope) by nailing on a bit of leather or other pliable material to act as a hinge. It is necessary to have a removable lid, firstly because one must muck-out the nit-ridden nests in the autumn, and secondly to see what is happening, a bird will not desert if it is looked at once or twice a sitting; in fact a spitting, hissing blue tit may frighten you more than you it.

When siting a box the three important considerations are predators, heat and the natural habitat.

All nests are liable to attract enemies, but it is obvious that some places are more accessible or eye-catching to cats, rats or vandals than are others. Even if the nest is built like a fortress, the bird is at risk when entering or leaving, and thus it should have somewhere to perch nearby so that it can look about. They also like to stand and sing near their nests, and fledglings prefer a twig to rest on after their first flight, rather than the whiskers of the cat waiting beneath.

Secondly, the nest must not be sited where the sun can shine on it: it can get so stifling in a box that the whole family can suffocate. I did not know this when I put up some house-martin prefabs. These were concrete imitations of the real thing, and are intended to encourage the martins to nest, and to discourage sparrows who cannot enlarge the entrances to fit their fat bodies; luckily the large eaves of the house shaded them.

The third important fact to consider when siting a nesting box is the height it should be above the ground. The lower it is, the more likely it is to be attacked by predators; on the other hand, robins and coal tits, for example, rarely nest above three foot, whilst it is pointless putting a nest at that height for blue tits as they will be looking for somewhere between five and ten feet. Other instinctive actions must be considered: birds which nest in woodland are not likely to be attracted to a box on a pole in the middle of a lawn and if they specialise in certain types of woodland, as coal tits do in conifer plantations, marsh tits in willow carrs and nuthatches in hawthorn thickets, then it helps to fit a box on the appropriate species of tree.

I do not like using nails on trees, I prefer to rest the box on a small branch and then tie it on to the trunk. The string rots after a year or so (plastic string, which does not, is usually too shiny and garish) but can be easily replaced. If ivy is allowed to grow up the tree it eventually holds the box in place.

Ivy is a controversial problem. My father says it is a sign of bad forestry, but I have heard that it does no harm in small amounts as it competes against its host only at root level. Certainly it is excellent as nesting cover for many small birds such as wrens or tits, and I therefore allow it in certain circumstances: never in the Formal Garden, or on trees with attractive bark, like birch, or with clean boles, like beech, or on young trees; but I do on some of the trees in the woodland, and in particular up the trunks of some dead elm near Nut Grove and a group of hawthorn near the End Ponds. There they make a dark grove of leafy columns which are doted on as nesting sites by insectivorous and water-loving birds.

I never allow any ivy to grow above twenty feet or its main stem to thicken more than an inch across.

Old man's beard, also known as traveller's joy because its former name had lewd connections for some of the more craftily minded Victorian ladies, is also good for nesting, and I find the mistle thrushes and blackbirds in particular like to nest high up in its tangle. This gives them an added incentive to sing from the tops of trees, and their songs go further.

Evergreens, apart from yew, are almost always attractive as a nesting site: our bushes of box and laurel are always full of nests, and chiff-chaffs and other low-nesters like those rows of miniature box which can be seen edging some kitchen gardens.

All hedges and thickets are also attractive, but above all the hawthorn is best, for not only do its thorns keep predators at bay, but also the forty-five degree angle from which its twigs and branches grow from each other is ideal for the foundation of most small nests. Hedges should not be too thick; a closely clipped holly or even hawthorn can become impenetrable. Some birds are very difficult to please, and everything must be in a site's favour before those birds will nest there. The long-tailed tit is one of these. (We call it the bottle tit locally, naming it after the shape of its nest which is domed over, has a hole near the top, and is packed with over a thousand feathers.) The worst mistake I made – from a bird's point of view – was to pull out the privet hedge which was growing between the poplars at the north of the Back Lawn. I did this in order to open the view into Nut Grove, but as the privet went, so I discovered amongst the uprooted shrubs the old remains of many nests, not only those of blackbirds, thrushes and finches, but also of bottle tits. I hoped that they would move to the adjacent blackthorn thicket, but I hoped in vain. However, they nest elsewhere in the wood and I often see their tiny magpie shapes undulating amongst the higher branches as they search for insects.

Apart from building nesting boxes, I have also tried to help birds start on their own by drilling holes in dead trees and stumps. I had thought that the holes, once started, would inspire the feathered chums to continue with the work. They utterly ignored these footling efforts.

Nowadays, because of my policy of planting well-spaced standards, an undergrowth of scrub quickly appears: mainly brambles and briar on the lowest level, topped by elder and thorn on the higher. I reinforce this growth with the planting of laurel, Lonicera Nitida and privet, and keep rides through it with the use of the Jungle-Buster. Nevertheless, this is still not as good for nesting as is a hedge, nor does it act, when in clump form, as a highway for all the little animals who use hedges as roads from one area to another. However, it is better than nothing. Once a year, in autumn, I cut a verge twelve foot wide along the south edge of the Beak and as a result, next spring, it is used for nesting by such grass lovers as partridges, peewits and larks: the grass is long enough to hide their nests, but short enough for their young.

The availability of food is important in attracting birds. Water is vital, and the chief reason for fatalities during an icy season can be lack of water rather than of food or warmth.

I have never made a bird table, but some Yorkshire friends commissioned a most extraordinary one, bristling with gadgets: springs to hold peanuts; spikes to hold lumps of fat; hooks to hang coconuts; special compartments for birds of different sizes; trays, shelves and baths; only lack of space prevented a changing room and a lavatory. A cock blackbird spent most of the time on the topmost perch chasing away the other birds.

I occasionally chuck bits of wet biscuit or pony food on the lawn, or hang up the remains of the Christmas turkey or the bone of a ham; once, when I had mumps, I hung a muslin bag full of fat outside my bedroom window. I lay in bed for three weeks, watching the tits pecking at the bag and feeling a twinge of sympathetic pain going through my vitals every time they did so. One of my less successful experiments was with a dead rabbit. I hung its corpse up near the back door, and the maggots duly appeared. They fell to the ground and were eaten by some of the less fastidious birds, such as starlings, whilst a spotted fly-catcher collected many of the flies' eggs off the rotting flesh. However, the whole thing stank like a banshee's armpit so I have not done it again.

I have concentrated on other methods of increasing the supply of bird food. Planting shrubs with the correct berries was an obvious thing to do, these have included snow-berries, viburnums, coton-easters, rowans and geans. Wild rice is apparently very good for grain-eating birds; I shall plant some next year.

As water attracts insects, and therefore insectivorous birds, so do dead trees. I have left a few of these standing in the woodland, where they are not offensively noticeable, and as a result often see the mouse-like shapes of tree creepers spiralling up and down the trunks – other birds can be mistaken for them, but the tree creeper is the only one who can walk down a tree. At least one pair of yaffles nest in the wood, by the number of holes there are likely to be more, unless our Mrs Yaffle has a "woman in a vinegar bottle" mentality and is always looking for somewhere better. Poplar wood burns badly, and therefore if I get any dead branches I do not saw them up for firewood, but put them on one of the big heaps I have hidden in the rough side of the Pinetum, there, obscured by the growth of privet and elder, the rotting timbers supply an abundant provision of insects and their grubs.

In many cases the diet of the birds is bad for the garden and during spring allotments all over the country are a-glitter and a-tinkle with milk bottle tops or streamers of silver paper on poles; with cut-out silhouettes of cats or hawks; fruit trees and bushes are festooned with nets and a-foam with bits of nylon waste; black threads zig-zag over patches of crocuses or primroses; whilst in the fields scarecrows, revolving vanes and time-guns continue the battle. I have been told that the best way to keep birds from a fruit tree is to hang a kipper on a branch. I do not know why this should work, perhaps it attracts cats, and certainly our cats keep some birds away from my vegetables – but nothing keeps them away from the big patch of crocus in front of the house, the forsythia and the hibiscus in the herbaceous borders, or the primroses in the glades.

★   ★   ★

BIRDS seen in the garden:
★nest found
†flying overhead

Blackbird★, 100, 148, 186–7
Blackcap
Bunting – reed, 151, 174
Bunting – yellow hammer★
Chaffinch★, 100, 173
Chiff-chaff★, 173, 186
Crow, 36
Cuckoo
Dab-chick★, 125, 174
Dove – collared★, 100, 174
Dove – ring
Dove – stock
Dove – turtle
Duck – carolina, 154, 171

Duck – chloe wigeon, 170
Duck – mallard★, 154, 173
Duck ★ muscovy, 15, 171
Duck – mandarin, 170
Duck – pin-tailed, 154
Duck – red-crested pochard, 154, 170
Duck – tufted, 154
Fieldfare, 153
Finch – bull
Finch – gold★
Finch – green★, 100
Fly-catcher – spotted★, 187
Goldcrest
Goose – Canada†

APPENDIX C

Invertebrates

Lists taken from the *News* of the British Butterfly Conservation Society.

WILD FLOWERS which provide a nectar-source from spring to autumn:

Primrose	Clover	Thistle
Pussy Willow	Hawkweed	Bramble
Dandelion	Lucerne	Majoram
Campion	Moon Daisy	Scabious
Garlic Mustard	Hemp Agrimony	Knapweed

GARDEN FLOWERS, in order of flowering through the summer, which are especially suitable for butterflies:

Polyanthus	Bugle	Aster
Alyssum	Mignonette	Verbena
Aubretia	Sweet William	Echium
Wallflower	Lavender	Cornflower
Thrift	Catmint	Heliotrope
Honesty	Phlox	Golden Rod
Sweet Rocket	Hyssop	Michaelmas Daisy
Valerian	Buddleia	Sedum

★　★　★

BUTTERFLIES recorded in Wastewood garden, 1981–82:

Blue, common	Copper, small	Skipper, Essex
Blue, holly	Orange tip	Skipper, large
Brimstone	Painted lady	Skipper, small
Brown, hedge	Peacock	Tortoise-shell, small
Brown, meadow	Purple hairstreak	White, large
Brown, wall	Red admiral	White, small
Comma	Ringlet	

*   *   *

MOTHS listed by the Colchester and Essex Museum:

Moth Trapping Evening at Wastewood, 31st July 1982

Weather conditions: warm and overcast, very slight intermittent breeze. Lamp on 9.00 pm to 12.45 am.

Mother-of-Pearl (micro)	Ruby tiger	Latticed heath
Yellow shell	Brown tail	Swallowtail
Dunbar	Garden dart	Spectacle
Flame shoulder	Mouse	Swallow prominent
Dark-barred twin spot carpet	Blood vein	Small phoenix
	Heart and dart	Hebrew character
Silver Y	China mark sp. (micro)	Buff arches
Large yellow underwing	Herald	Lime speck pug
Alder kitten	Antler	Knotgrass
Lunar spotted pinion	Scorched carpet	Small square spot
Smokey wainscot	Dusky sallow	Least yellow underwing
Common footman	Clouded border	Poplar hawk
Lesser yellow underwing	Common pug	July highflyer
Early thorn	Garden pebble (micro)	Willow beauty
Shuttle-shaped dart	Peppered moth (melanic)	Scalloped hazel
Light emerald	Small waved umber	Clay
Brimstone	Broad-bordered yellow underwing?	Scalloped oak
Marbled minor?		Straw dot
Small fan-footed wave	Nutmeg	Straw underwing
Tawny speckled pug	Dot	Lackey
Common wainscot	Common rustic	
Magpie	Purple bar	
Brown-line bright eye	Coxcomb prominent	64 species.

Other microlepidoptera specimens taken for identification purposes.

Other records:
Philoscia muscorum (woodlouse), *Ananeus umbraticus* (spider).

*   *   *

General list of INVERTEBRATES:

Microlepidoptera to Light (C.N.H.S.) Collected 31st July, 1982.

Agriphila straminella (D. & S.)
Scoparia ambigulais (Treit.)
★Cydia splendana (Hb.)
Clepsis spectrana (Treit.)
★Croesia forsskaleana (L.)
Cnephasia incertana (Treit.)
Brachmia rufescens (Haw.)
Cnephasia interjectana (Haw.)
Nemapogon cloacella (Haw.)
Cnephasia longana (Haw.)
Yponomeuta evonymella (L.)

★Catoptria falsella (D. & S.)
Neofriseria singula (Stdgr.)
★Spilonota ocellana (D. & S.)
Pandemis heparana (D. & S.)
Agapeta hamana (L.)
★Phycita roborella (D. & S.)
★Nymphula nympheata (L.), (Brown China Mark)
Eurrhypara coronata (Hufn.)
Agriphila tristella (D. & S.)

Notes

Yponomeuta evonymella – "rare in the county." This is only recent north Essex record. May be a vagrant to Britain.
Catoptria falsella – a moss feeder, "very local and rare."
Neofriseria singula – "very locally common."
★New 10 kilometre square records.
All determinations by A. M. Emmet, February, 1983.

Alder fly
Ant
Aphid
Bee, bumble, 178
Bee, honey
Beetle, bark
Beetle, cardinal, 111
Beetle, devil's coach horse
Beetle, giant diving, 134
Beetle, ladybird, 111
Beetle, tortoise, 112
Beetle, wasp
Beetle, water, 174
Beetle, whirlygig, 133, 174
Caddis fly, 134, 173
Cricket, 178
Damsel fly, common blue, 134
Dragon fly, hawker, 112, 134

Drone fly, 120
Ear-wig
Froghopper
Froghopper, large, 111
Grasshopper, 178
Hornet
Hover fly, 111
Ichneuman fly, 112–3
Infusora
Lace wing
Molluscs
  – Mussel, swan, 74, 134
  – Slug, 75, 170
  – Snail, banded, 74
     eared, 134
     garden, 74–5
     marsh, 134
     ramshorn, 134, 173
     wandering, 134

Mosquito, 55
Pede, centi-
Pede, milli-, 178
Spider, orb, 112
Spider, parachute, 112
Springtail
Thrip
Tubifex, 135
Wasp, common, 193
Wasp, gall, 94
Wasp, wood, 111
Water boatman, 133–4
Water cyclop, 173
Water mite, 134, 173
Water skate, 133
Woodlouse
Worm, 92

APPENDIX D1

Flora, wild

Having decided to record all the flora in the garden and having ticked off all the easy ones in my Keble Martin, like water lily and dandelion, I began to notice previously ignored plants; some of these were ones which, although large, had insignificant flowers like the dyer's greenweed or weld: three feet high with neat spires of green flowers. It used to be grown locally as a crop, but makes a feeble dye if my experiments were anything to go by: I boiled a handkerchief with a saucepan of leaves for two hours and the result was a barely noticeable yellow stain; perhaps the sprinkling of salt that Dominie absent-mindedly added to it as she bustled past the stove had some adverse effect.

Another previously ignored plant was the figwort, also three feet high but with flowers like tiny green and maroon coal scuttles; it is one of the few plants pollinated by wasps.

I had missed some plants because they had been too low growing: fumitory, possibly so named because its delicate leaves and stems look like blue-grey smoke puffing from the ground, the tiny white stars of mouse-eared chickweed and scarlet pimpernel – I had not known that its flowers fold up in the dark.

Even the more noticeable flowers repaid a closer inspection, particularly the St John's worts. We have at least three species in the garden, the common, the square stemmed and the hairy, and like the garden varieties they have bright golden petals from the centre of which bursts forth a corona of bright stamens, hence the fact that their local names often associate them with the sun.

The garden is extremely well equipped with violets. These can hybridise, so my identifications may be inaccurate; none of them seem to conform to the descriptions in the reference books although some of them seem to come close to the common violet (scented blue-purple flowers), the woodland violet (lilac, shade-loving flowers) and the sweet violet, variety dumetorum (white, with a red-purple spur: but mine do not smell, the description says they should). The first-named grow everywhere, but mainly as surprising seedlings in parts of the Formal Garden, the white violets speckle the ground around the birches of the Silver Garden, and the Pinetum and the Aspen grove have groups of the woodland type violets which show their bright lilac patches well against the background of the ground-hugging ivy. I have transplanted a few violets to sites under oak trees in the no doubt pitiful hope that this will help to rear the silver-washed fritillaries whose caterpillar life starts on oaks, from which they fall to continue on violets, and up which they climb to turn into chrysalises in the crevices of the oak bark. Most other fritillaries are also reared on violets.

A group of flowers which attracted me because of possible rarities was the pea family, the rarities being the hairy vetchling, a two foot high plant with pale blue and crimson flowers, and the fyfield pea which has large, deep pink flowers and lumpy, hooked pods like taloned arthritic fingers. Both of these only grow naturally within forty miles of us; needless to say, I have found neither in the garden, but I have discovered, during my searches, what a large and varied family this group of plants is. One of the most noticeable is the black medick, not noticeable for its tiny yellow flowers which grow in bunches no bigger than a lentil, but for the places where it grows: it is usually the first plant to appear on the bare soil that has been exposed by any deep digging. As some of the areas I cleared had not been touched for fifty years, this suggests that the black medick has great powers of germination over long periods of dormancy. Turrill says that the seeds of the kidney vetch last longer than any other British plant, for about ninety years, but I would have thought the poppy lasted longer: it often appears on the newly excavated verges of roads and of course everyone knows what happened to the bomb craters of Flanders fields.

One of the prettiest of my vetches is the tufted vetch, which can climb up to six feet and has plumes of blue-purple flowers. The common birdsfoot trefoil is also very pretty, with its bunches of yellow flowers like brilliant bananas, so noticeable that it has over seventy local names throughout Britain.

The flowers of the tare are so small that they are ignored unless one does a bit of "swooping earthwards" to see the sparse sprinkling of the isolated blue flowers which grow to an almost fluffy mass of stems and leaves. I could never understand the fuss that the Bible made of this humble weed until I tried to put my scythe through the wiry tangle of a tare patch.

Smell can be much more evocative than any of the other senses: I have found myself when walking past a spice shop in the drabber part of Bradford suddenly transported back to the hot, bustling, dusty, shouting streets of Cairo and of Lagos; the open door of a Greek restaurant has sent me dreaming of the time I lay along the bow-sprit of a great ketch, with the wine-dark sea glassy below me and the white walls of a small Aegean harbour silently approaching in the warm twilight; occasionally, as I shuffle through knee-high drifts of rustling autumn leaves I am sent back through the years when I waded through the woods of my childhood.

One of the most evocative of these smells is a sharp, bitter-sweet scent which occurs whenever I tramp through the damper parts of the garden. In spring and early summer they are crowded with the little spires of bugle, a plant which can grow up to nine inches in height and whose blue floral spikes are set about with purple tinged leaves. I later realised that the smaller spikes which grew amongst the bugle were of an entirely different plant, ground ivy, and it was this which exuded the scent from its crushed leaves; not surprising, for it is of the same family as mint, marjoram, thyme, cat mint and balm.

Perhaps the most attractive of the wild plants in the garden is one with no noticeable smell and with dull little flowers: its attraction comes during the autumn. The black bryony grows from a tuber; I have found several of these when digging banks away in the Silver Garden, and the large, white, poisonous lumps of yeasty growth look almost sinister, like the hibernating young of some malevolent animal. The tiny flowers are greenish, but they turn into glowing red berries; the heart-shaped leaves, in their turn, become bright yellow, and the two contrasting and vivid colours twine spirally up the trunks of trees, or weave amongst the hedges, like golden necklaces strung with rubies.

★   ★   ★

FLORA
Indigenous Plants

Cyclamen

APPENDIX D2

Flora, introduced

ROSES

SPECIES

Of all roses, the most noticeable, and to me, the most pleasant, are the species: large bushy plants of great variety of shape, flower, foliage and even of thorn. Some of Dominie's most successful choices include:

Canary Bird: bright yellow flowers on six-foot arching stems.

Blanc Double de Coubert: grass-green leaves, large white flowers like bunches of tissue paper, a superb and very strong scent.

Nevada: floppy white flowers about four inches across; our bush was a very fast grower to eight feet.

Moyesii Geranium: small crimson flowers, long – 3 inches – bottle-shaped hips; our twelve foot high shrub has a very upright growth, more like a bamboo clump than a rose bush.

Sericea Pteracantha: the flowers are small and white and have only four petals, the thorns are large and, when young, of a translucent scarlet which glows vividly when the sun shines through, so do not make my mistake and plant them in the half-shade.

Rubrifolia: the flowers are pinkish-mauve, the stems are reddish-brown, the leaves are a smokey bluish-green, the bright hips shiny and profuse, it is thus interesting throughout the year.

Frühlingsgold: cream flowers with golden centres, a hand-width across, strong scent of wild rose; perhaps because it is the nearest to the Pinetum ours grew rapidly and then began to ail.

Frühlingsmorgen: flowers pale pink shading to cream at centre, long stems, wild rose scent.

Frau Dagmar Hartopp: rose-pink, a smaller bush than average, huge hips like tomatoes.

Frau Karl Druschki: white, very large flowers with no scent; it was not considered patriotically named in the first world war and was rechristened *White Swan*, but the new name was forgotten after the return of peace.

Gallica: also called the *French Rose*, the *Apothecaries Rose*, the *Rose of Lancaster*; red, a very old and ancestral species.

Rosa Mundi: light crimson streaked with white, also very old, said to be named after the Fair Rosamund who was the mistress of Henry II and poisoned by his wife Eleanor of Aquitaine. One feels that the author of the epitaph on her tomb must have been a morbid and unpleasant person:

Hic jacet in tomba rose mundi, non rose munda,
Non redolet, sed olet, quae redolere solet.
[This tomb doth here enclose
The world's most beautiful rose,
Rose passing sweet erewhile
Now nought but odour vile.]   (Southey)

Ours is very prone to mildew.

SHRUBS

These are particularly fine on the Back Lawn where they stand-in as rhododendrons, which we cannot grow. Unfortunately, as they are smaller than rhododendrons, and not evergreen, nettles and other tall weeds can grow through them if not controlled. Dominie chose:

Buff Beauty: apricot-yellow, a low shrub of less than five foot, but it spreads widely with dark, arching stems.

Constance Spry: clear pink, red-tinted young foliage, strong scent of myrrh.

Madame Pierre Oger: white, pink or red, depending on the weather, very pretty double flowers, dark thorns, bush over six foot.

Roseraie de l'Hay: rich purple, peony-like flowers, densely-growing shrub.

Wedding Day: cream, tinged pink, the profuse flowers have pointed petals; it is a rambler.

CLIMBERS

The climbers put against the walls of the house and the out-buildings include:

Danse de Feu: large, orange-red flowers, long flowering season.

Pink Perpetue: carmine buds changing to clear pink double flowers.

Golden Showers: golden to cream flowers four inches across.

Handel: long flowering, creamy-white flowers edged with red.

Madame Alfred Carriere: she grows very well on our sheltered north wall, her white flowers tap eerily with ghost hands at our bedroom windows.

Seagull: another white, very small flowers in vast profusion, the most dramatic of all our climbers, even beating . . .

Filipes "kiftsgate": this Dominie planted against a pear tree by the shrub roses, it now gives a pleasant vertical contrast to the rounded domes of the bushes. It is probably the best climber for growing in semi-wild conditions up trees or sheds; the cascades of small but heavily scented white flowers now pour fifteen feet down the branches of the pear tree, I have been told that it will get as high as 30 feet.

FLORIBUNDAS

We have a variety of these, the most noticeable being:

Africa Star: mauve

Elizabeth of Glamis: salmon-pink.

Ma Perkins: shell-pink.

The Queen Elizabeth: pink.

Sea Pearl: pink.

Iceberg: white. My first enthusiasm for this has become dampened, its dead petals hang on and make an unsightly bush.

HYBRID TEA

Of all ours, the only failure, in my opinion but not in Dominie's, is **Blue Moon**. Most rose breeders, apparently, are besotted with the idea of producing a blue rose and to me the results are dingy effects in mauves and greys.

FLOWERS

Some of the most pleasant or interesting acquisitions mentioned on page 86 include:

Layia Elegans (*fried eggs* or *tidy tips*): annual. Given to me by Mrs Pillweed, who had suffered the chagrin of living for many years under the title "not yet the oldest person in the parish". The disappointment of bearing this inferior position for so long had made her snappish and morose; luckily I caught her in one of her kindlier moods as she had just heard that her superior in years had caught 'flu. The flowers have bright yellow centres with white-tipped petals, they seed well.

Gypsophila (*baby's breath*): annual. The wiry grey stems bear a cloud of small white flowers which make it look like a miniature snow storm. Given to me by Mabel Plum; her father was my great-grandfather's butler over a hundred years ago. (She also gave me his recipe book for wines and punches, most of which are in the opulent vein of: "Take four bottles of brandy, 2 of claret, a pound of sugar and one nutmeg . . .")

Geranium Phaeum (*dusky cranesbill, mournful widow*): perennial. It is odd that black or near-black flowers are even more eye-catching than white ones, hence the efforts, mainly unsuccessful, to breed black roses and tulips. This plant is wild, but is also planted in gardens. I was given it by a farming friend who has it by the front door of his Elizabethan farm-house. There it looks impressive and is a good contrast to the silvery leaved plants he has growing in the dry area below his overhanging first floor: mine has been planted between two specie roses and looks too insignificant as a result.

Crambe Cordifolia (*ornamental seakale*): perennial. A multitudinous swarm of small white flowers hovers over the huge green leaves. The whole plant is about six foot by six foot: the only thing that I have against it is its name – I was often fed seakale as a child and it repulsed me, now, thank goodness, it is rare and expensive as a vegetable. Given to me by "Never-Sweat" Siskins, whose wife grew it in their garden.

Sedum: perennial. The weaver who gave it to me called it the *Ice Plant* because it is always cold. His dozen leaves, stuck in the herbacious border, are now large ugly clumps of pinkish flowers, their virtue is in attracting butterflies; the *Autumn Sedum*, which we bought later, and which is even uglier, being puce, does not even seem to attract insects.

Nigella(*love-in-a-mist*): annual. Hart gave us this. It has beautiful sky-blue flowers which are surrounded by feathery green ruffs. Best planted in clumps to make a fuzzy mass.

Onopordon Arabicum (*scotch thistle*): perennial. As it grows about 8 foot high, has silvery leaves and purple heads, it looks magnificent at the back of a herbaceous border, beside any dark-leaved plants. It seeds easily like most thistles, and not always where it is wanted; Amos Cuthedge of the Seven Tailors, who gave it to me, said his neighbours were always grumbling about its appearance in their gardens.

Borago Officinalis (*borage*): annual. Very pretty blue flowers which contrast well with their dark, hairy leaves, they also look nice floating in a glass of Pimms. Given to me by old Swallow, the village baker. (He used to jog around in a pony trap, laying a scented trail of newly baked bread. Every Armistice day he would parade into church with the rest of the British Legion and his tiny stooped frame was a-glitter and a-tinkle with medals and ribbons. Brigadier Goodey used to read out the words:

"They shall not grow old as we that are left grow old. Age shall not weary them, nor the years condemn . . ."

Swallow would stand stiffly to attention, his eyes gazing into the past, crying bitterly.)

Viola (*garden gates*): perennial. There are many species of viola and true species may be scarce in gardens. This came from the garden of a little weather-boarded cottage, a garden which was a random riot of hollyhocks and cabbages, pansies and beans, carrots and daisies and all the other flowers and vegetables which can be expected in an old country garden. "Noteless Nora", who lived there, gave me a handful of violas which she ripped from her onion patch: they are very small, less than an inch across, and of the most vivid and deep violet. They have spread abundantly. Noteless Nora was so called because of her amiable simplicity. Bell, who lived near her, came into our kitchen one day, chuckling, "A couple of city gents came to visit old Nora today and I heard one say; 'I've come to introduce you to Jesus'. Nora took a look at the other fella and gave him a little curtsey and said 'I've heard ever so much about you.'"

Macleaya (*plume poppy*): perennial. The feathery spikes of pale flowers atop 7 foot stems are slightly insignificant; the interest is in the very attractive leaves which are somewhat like fig leaves in shape but with lobes that are much more scalloped, glaucous blue above with prominent veins, pale grey beneath. (Mr Wrekin who gave them to me has an abundance of frogs in his small pond: every year he swaps some of these for some of my newts. By the negative results, we suspect that they then walk through the village back to their respective homes.)

Salvia Sclarea "turkestanica": perennial: This is a tall plant (4 to 5 foot) with strange pinkish-white flowers shaped rather like the gaping beak of a parrot. Its speciality is its odour.

"Run your hands over its leaves, and then smell them," said Mrs Rutland. I did so, and was instantly transported back to the changing rooms of my school sports pavilion, the sleeping quarters of Chelsea Barracks, and various deb dances.

"I know the smell," I said broodingly, "but I can't place it."

"Sweat," she said firmly.

It smells of sweat very strongly, and therefore it is an amusing plant to have as it is one of the few which actually meets the advertising slogan so often met in gardening magazines – ". . . it will amaze your friends . . ."

Mrs Rutland gave me this, and many other plants; some of these she had received from friends who, in their turn, had got them from their friends. Another one was . . .

Asperula odorata (*sweet woodruff*): Rhizomatous. This is a fairly common wild flower in chalky woodlands, a relation of goosegrass; but it did not grow in my garden and Mrs Rutland planted some near the rabbit warren, where it is very pleasant, showing whorls of small white flowers and smelling of newly mown hay.

Prunus Tenella (*dwarf Russian almond*): shrub. This spreads as a well-spaced group of thin, wiry suckers, each about two feet high. The flowers are light pink, on the bare springtime wands. It grows well on chalk and amidst rock-gardens; ours does not do so well as I planted it in the overlong grass beside the Near Pond. Given to me by "Hot Hands" Honeyball, the parish Romeo who, much to the surprise of the village, gave up a long and successful career of lechery to marry a farmworker's shy daughter and become a besotted husband, devoted father and energetic gardener.

GROUND-COVER PLANTS

We planted about thirty different flowers and shrubs as a result of Mr Barcock's visit, some of the most effective weed smotherers amongst these are:

Spanish gorse: our three tiny plants, placed dubiously in a triangle five feet apart according to the instructions, have now merged to form one single mound about three foot high and four yards across.

It looks like a soft, fluffy ottoman, but the spines, on closer inspection, are numerous and sharp; spiders seem to like it above all plants for their nurseries. The flowers are yellow. No weed has beaten it except for the occasional bell bine – these are painted with weedkiller.

Hydrangea white wave: I have never liked either pink or blue hydrangeas, though I cannot explain why I think their colours so unpleasant; the only time I thought any attractive was in Madeira, where some of the mountain lanes are bordered by blue hydrangeas in magnificent array. However, I like the white varieties and I chose white wave partly because it is a reasonable weed smotherer, also because its flat lace caps look well in a pond setting, but mainly because Mr Barcock said it was the best type he had which would grow well under trees; the cuttings I took from the one in the herbaceous border now flower strikingly in some of the darker corners of the Mangrove Swamp.

Hypericum Hidcote: all the St John's worts have beautiful flowers; this has golden, waxy ones on a bush which spreads freely by suckers and grows four feet high.

Prunus Otto Luyken: when planted in the same way as the Spanish gorse it is almost as good as weedkiller. The narrow leaves are evergreen, the candles of white flowers contrast well with them.

Viburnum Opulus and Sterile: all vibernums grow well in our soil, these have reached nine feet. The opulus is a domesticated form of the guelder rose which grows wild in the wood, it is also known as the water elder and like the hydrangea mentioned above looks attractive beside a pond; the cuttings I took now reflect their white pancakes in the waters of the Near Pond. The latter viburnum is the snowball tree, and its round balls of white flowers look very striking against the background of the beech hedge.

Cranesbill: we bought several varieties of these, they all have the ability to spread well, the pretty flowers range in colour from blues to pinks to reds, they average a foot in height and some have leaves which smell pleasant when crushed during weedings or transplants.

ORNAMENTAL GRASSES

My interest in ornamental grasses is not echoed by Dominie who does not care for them much, in fact she has a quirky loathing for pampas grass, but the clumps I have planted merge well in certain parts of the garden, particularly by the Near Pond, and so compromise by looking beautiful to me without being intrusively irritating to Dominie.

I planted my first selection by buying a few different packets and pressing the contents into the ground in certain chosen sights. This was during my "crassly optimistic" period, and none came up; they seem to need as much delicate nurturing as any other exotic plant. My second attempt was more successful, our friend Mark, who lived in the Park, telephoned me and said that as he was selling his house I should hurry round and dig up what I wanted. The most attractive of these include:

Stipa Gigantea: the four to five foot stems are like rods of greenish-brown glass, they arch under the airy weight of large, metallic looking seed heads, these open and close slightly as the atmospheric humidity changes.

Quaking grass: its slightly hoplike heads are all of a tremble in the slightest wind, they make an intriguing little mobile patch.

Gardener's garters: this spreads well, but perhaps the blue-green leaves, with their creamy-white longitudinal stripes, are a little more eye-catching than Dominie likes.

Koeleria Gracilis: the flowers are creamy-white in dense, bottle-brush-like spikes, they are about two foot high and, like the narrow blue-green leaves, they arch outwards from the centre.

*　　*　　*

TREES
Introduced Plants

Abies Grandis – silver fir, 96
Abies Koreana – Korean fir, 96
Acer Platanoides – Norway maple, 108
Acer Pseudoplatanus brilliantissimum
　– brilliant sycamore, 105–6
Acer Rubrum – red maple, 102
Aesculus Hippocastanum – horse
　chestnut
Aesculus Indica – Indian horse
　chestnut, 106
Alnus Glutinosa – alder, 95, 108, 110
Betula
　Ermanii, 95
　Jacquemontii, 95
　Papyrifera – paper birch, 99
　Pendula fastigata – fastigiate birch,
　103

Pendula Youngii – Young's
　weeping birch, 99, 100
Utilis – Himalayan birch, 99
Carpinus Betulus – hornbeam, 95,
　108, 110
Carpinus Betulus Fastigiata – fastigiate
　hornbeam, 103
Castanea Sativa – sweet chestnut, 105
Cedrus Deodara – deodar cedar
Chamaecyparis Lawsoniana – Lawson
　cypress
Chamaecyparis Lawsoniana Allumii,
　86
Chamaecyparis Lawsoniana
　Columnaris
Chamaecyparis Lawsoniana
　Kilmacurragh

Ulmus Glabra Pendula – weeping wych elm

Ulmus Rubra Dicksonii – Dickson's golden elm.

★   ★   ★

SHRUBS
Introduced Plants

Abutilon Vitifolium
Azalea, 54
Berberis "firefly" – barberry
Berberis Thunbergii Atropurpurea Superba – barberry
Buddleia Davidii – buddlea, 86, 190
Buddleia "black night" – buddlea
Buddleia Fallowiana – buddlea
Buxus Sempervirens – box, 100, 146, 186
Buxus Suffriticosa – edging box, 186
Camellia Elegans, 83–4
Ceanothus – Californian lilac, 86
Chaenomeles Maulei – ornamental quince
Chimonanthus Praecox – wintersweet, 102
Clematis
  Macropetala, 86
  Montana
  Mrs Chomondeley
  Stellata, 44
  Ville de Lyone
Cornus Alba Elegantissima – dogwood
Cornus Kousa – dogwood
Cornus Stolonifera – dogwood
Corylus Avelcana "Kentish cob" – hazel, 160, 215
Corylus Avelcana "Pearson's prolific", 160, 215
Corylus Maxima – filbert, 160, 215
Corylus Maxima – filbert frizzled, 215
Cotoneaster "firebird"
Cotoneaster "Horizontalis"
Cotoneaster "Lactea"
Cotoneaster "Simonsii", 31–2, 187
Cydonia Oblonga – quince, 159
Cystus Burkwoodii – broom, 37–9
Cystus Decumbens – broom
Daphne Odora
Deutzia Gracilis Rosea
Deutzia Scabra
Eunonymus Alatus "Red cascade" –

winged spindle
Forsythia Fortunei, 188
Fuchsia
Garrya Elliptica – tassel bush
Genista hispanica – Spanish gorse, 206–7
Hydrangea
  "Hatfield rose"
  "King George"
  "Presioza"
  "White wave", 207
  Petiolaris – climbing hydrangea
Hypericum Calycinum – Rose of Sharon
Hypericum Patulum "Hidcote" – St John's wort, 207
Jasminum Nudiflorum – winter jasmine, 41, 44
Lavendula Spica – old English lavender, 190
Laurus Nobilis – bay, 59, 159
Ligustrum Ovalifolium – garden privet
Lonicera Americana – honeysuckle, 39
Mahonia Pinnata
Paeony Lutea Ludlowii – tree peony
Passiflora Caerulea – passion flower, 81
Philadelphus Virginal – mock orange, 25
Polygonum Baldschuanicum – Russian vine
Potentilla "Katherine Dykes"
Prunus Laurocerasus – Common laurel
Prunus Laurocerasus Magnoliaefolia, 29
Prunus Laurocerasus "Otto Luyken", 207
Prunus Tenella – dwarf Russian almond, 206
Pyrancantha Coccinea Lalandii – firethorn
Rhus Typhina – stag's horn sumach

★   ★   ★

FLOWERS *etc*

Introduced Plants

APPENDIX E

Food

The following are the fruit trees which we grow in the garden as a result of Hart's advice (his opinions are bracketed):

APPLES (in order of plucking):
Culinary:
Early Victoria (Heavy cropper of bright green fruit.)
Grenadier (Delicious fruit, but as they do not keep must be cooked from the tree.)
Lane's Prince Albert (Large green fruit, striped red; white, juicy flesh, cooks "fluffy".)
Bramley Seedling (The best of all cooking apples, about the largest, too. Very big tree; needs pollination.)
Monarch (Keeps in the larder until spring; frost-resistant blossom; a "solid" apple.)
Newton Wonder (Biennial; pale green with scarlet stripes.)

Dessert:
Beauty of Bath (Pretty, highly coloured fruit, they should be picked and eaten early; crisp flesh.)
Tydeman's Early Worcester (Not as sweet as the Pearmain, but matures earlier.)
James Greive (Blooms early, upright tree; good pollinator; rich-flavoured fruit.)
Worcester Pearmain (Attractive fruit, conical and crimson; crisp; best off the tree rather than stored.)
Cox's Orange Pippin (The "king" of apples, superb taste; delicate tree.)

Miller's Seedling (Heavy bearer, even on chalk; small fruit.)
Laxton's Superb (Heavy cropper; sweet, juicy fruit).
Egremont Russet (Smallish tree; heavy cropper of excellent fruit.)
D'Arcy Spice (Our local tree; fruit almost "nutty", greenish-bronze; sweeter if eaten after Christmas.)
Sturmer Pippin (Also a local; fruit tastes slightly of gooseberry; good keeper, hangs on tree till December.)

PLUMS:
Greengage (I think the best of all plums, very juicy and sweet. It is a reluctant bearer unless pollinated with . . .)
Victoria (The most versatile and "plum-like" of plums.)
Cullins's Golden Gage (Excellent both raw and bottled.)
Laxton's Gage (Heavy bearer; large tree.)
Prune Damson (Very hardy tree; fruit like a small, dark plum.)

NUTS:
Filbert Frizzled (Long, superbly tasting nuts.)
Kentish Cob (Heavy bearer of large nuts.)
Pearson's Prolific (Small bush, but large round nuts.)

★   ★   ★

A RECIPE FOR A COMPOST HEAP
1 Select a site near a birch tree, as the myrrchosal fungus round its roots will accelerate the processes of decay.
2 Remove the turf to expose the bare ground. Any length will do, but the width should be limited between 6' to 13'; the ultimate height of the heap should be between 3' to 6'.
3 Put on alternate layers of compost and soil, both 3' thick.
4 After the heap is 1' high, you can insert bio-dynamic preparations made to speed up the process.
5 Cover temporarily, between each topping–up, with sacks or straw.
6 Finish with an overcoat of porous soil or straw.
7 Keep moist, but not waterlogged (if the soil is liable to excess moisture, a brushwood drain should have been built).
8 Turn the heap after three to five months.
9 Plough or dig in within three hours of removal, it rapidly loses its goodness if left to weather on the surface of the ground.

Bibliography

NATURAL HISTORY
Britain's Structure and Scenery,
Sir Dudley Stamp; Collins (New Naturalist No. 4), 1970.
Natural History of the British Isles,
Country Life Books/Hamlyn Publishing Group, 1979.
Natural History and Antiquities of Selborne,
Gilbert White, 1788; Macmillan, 1911.
Plant and Planet,
A. Huxley; Allen Lane, 1974.
British Plant Life,
W. B. Turrill; Collins (New Naturalist No. 10), 1948.
The Natural History of the Garden,
Michael Chinnery; Collins, 1977.

GARDENING
The Gardener's Golden Treasury, with *Sanders Encyclopaedia of Gardening*,
Revised by A. G. L. Hellyer; Collingridge, 1895/1964.
The Dictionary of Garden Plants in Colour,
Roy Hay & M. Synge Patrick; RHS/Ebury Press/Michael Joseph, 1969.
The Reader's Digest Complete Library of the Garden (3 Vols),
The Reader's Digest Assn, 1963.
The Wild Garden,
Judith Berrisford; Faber, 1966.

Wild Flowers for the Garden,
Stephen Dealler; Batsford, 1977.
Collins Guide to Roses,
B. Park; Collins, 1956.
The Old Shrub Roses,
Graham Stuart Thomas; Phoenix, 1956.
Down the Garden Path,
Beverley Nichols; Jonathan Cape, 1932.
Garden open Today,
Beverley Nichols; Cape, 1963.

TREES
The Trees of Great Britain & Ireland (7 vols),
H. J. Elwes & A. Henry; Edinburgh, privately printed, 1906.
Trees and Shrubs Hardy for the British Isles (4 vols),
W. J. Bean; John Murray, 1914.
Shrubs and Trees for the Garden,
A. Osborn; Ward Lock, 1931.
Hilliers Manual of Trees and Shrubs,
David & Charles, 1972.
A Field Guide to the Trees of Britain & Northern Europe,
A. Mitchell; Collins, 1974.
Forestry Commission Bulletin:
    No. 14 "Forestry practice".
    No. 15 "Know your Conifers".
    No. 20 "Know your Broadleaves".
    No. 29 "Wildlife conservation in Woodlands".
    No. 30 "Exotic Forest trees in Great Britain".
Practical Forestry for the Agent & Surveyor,
C. E. Hart; the Estates Gazette, 1967.
The Forester's Companion,
N. D. G. James; Basil Blackwell, 1955.
Trees, Woods and Man,
H. L. Edlin; Collins (New Naturalist No. 32), 1956.

FLORA
The Concise British Flora in Colour,
W. Keble Martin; Elbury Press/Michael Joseph, 1965.
Finding Wild Flowers,
R. S. R. Fitter; Collins, 1971.

Wild Flowers,
John Gilmour & Max Walters; Collins (New Naturalist No. 5), 1954.
Flora of Essex,
Stanley T. Jermyn; Essex Naturalist's Trust, 1974.
Hedges,
E. Pollard, M. D. Hooper, N. W. Moore; Collins (New Naturalist No. 58), 1974.
Grass and Grasslands,
Ian Moore; Collins (New Naturalist No. 48), 1966.
The Observer Book of Grasses, Sedges and Rushes,
Francis Rose; Frederick Warne, 1974.
The Oxford Book of Flowerless Plants,
Oxford, 1966.
Food for Free,
Richard Mabey; Collins, 1972.

FAUNA

A Field Guide to the Insects of Britain & Northern Europe,
Michael Chinery; Collins, 1972.
The Oxford Book of Insects,
John Burton; Oxford, 1968.
Insect Natural History,
A. D. Imms; Collins (New Naturalist No. 8), 1947.
British Birds,
F. B. Kirkman & F. C. R. Jourdain; Nelson, 1930.
Woodland Birds,
Eric Simms; Collins (New Naturalist No. 52), 1971.
The Oxford Book of Vertebrates,
D. Whiteley & M. Nixon; Oxford, 1972.

GENERAL

The Importance of Living,
Lin Yutang; Heinemann, 1938.
Primrose McConnell's Agricultural Notebook,
Edited by Dr Ian Moore; Newnes–Butterworths, 1833/1976.
Steps,
Robert Graves; Cassell, 1958.
The Garden, Journal of the Royal Horticultural Society.

Oasis, The magazine of Wildlife Gardening and Conservation.
News, The magazine of the British Butterfly Conservation Society.
The Field.